Nordic Food Transitions

The ambition of this book is to investigate a possible transition in the markets for food in the Nordic countries. Six chapters from various disciplinary traditions study change and innovation within the food sectors in Denmark, Sweden and Norway; while an introductory chapter discusses the findings of these analyses. Specialty food has established a strong position within product categories such as craft beer in Denmark and organic food in Sweden, but has failed to do so in others. The emergence of markets for specialty foods have been promoted by top-down policy initiatives and bottom-up entrepreneurial efforts. Far from providing the only relevant platform for food transition and innovation, the "New Nordic Food" manifesto has helped creating a territorialized action space for networks of food producers and distributors promoting diversity in local food and rural development. Some of the specialty food networks have succeeded in re-scaling their operations from a local to a national market. Today even large retailers and food processing companies have to pay notice to the ongoing changes among consumers. There is however a paradoxical constraint in a transition towards specialty food. A large-scale transition would imply that producers and consumers abandon precisely what constitute them – their exclusiveness.

The chapters in this book were originally published as a special issue of *European Planning Studies*.

Jesper Manniche is a Senior Research Fellow experienced within a range of research fields related to rural development including local food networks, innovation and knowledge creation, small businesses and entrepreneurship, and regional governance and policy.

Bjørnar Sæther is Professor of Human Geography with a specialization in economic geography. His teaching and research activities are related to resource based industries, innovation in rural areas and sustainability issues.

Nordic Food Transitions

Towards a Territorialized Action Space for Food and Rural Development

Edited by
Jesper Manniche and Bjørnar Sæther

LONDON AND NEW YORK

First published 2018
by Routledge
2 Park Square, Milton Park, Abingdon, Oxon, OX14 4RN, UK

and by Routledge
711 Third Avenue, New York, NY 10017, USA

Routledge is an imprint of the Taylor & Francis Group, an informa business

© 2018 Taylor & Francis

All rights reserved. No part of this book may be reprinted or reproduced or utilised in any form or by any electronic, mechanical, or other means, now known or hereafter invented, including photocopying and recording, or in any information storage or retrieval system, without permission in writing from the publishers.

Trademark notice: Product or corporate names may be trademarks or registered trademarks, and are used only for identification and explanation without intent to infringe.

British Library Cataloguing in Publication Data
A catalogue record for this book is available from the British Library

ISBN 13: 978-1-138-49323-0

Typeset in Minion Pro
by RefineCatch Limited, Bungay, Suffolk

Publisher's Note
The publisher accepts responsibility for any inconsistencies that may have arisen during the conversion of this book from journal articles to book chapters, namely the possible inclusion of journal terminology.

Disclaimer
Every effort has been made to contact copyright holders for their permission to reprint material in this book. The publishers would be grateful to hear from any copyright holder who is not here acknowledged and will undertake to rectify any errors or omissions in future editions of this book.

Contents

Citation Information   vii
Notes on Contributors   ix

1. Introduction: Emerging Nordic food approaches   1
   Jesper Manniche and Bjørnar Sæther

2. Quality turns in Nordic food: a comparative analysis of specialty food in Denmark, Norway and Sweden   11
   Henrik Halkier, Laura James and Egil Petter Stræte

3. Sustainability transformations in the balance: exploring Swedish initiatives challenging the corporate food regime   29
   Jacob von Oelreich and Rebecka Milestad

4. How relationships can influence an organic firm's network identity   47
   Gunn-Turid Kvam, Hilde Bjørkhaug and Ann-Charlott Pedersen

5. It's never too late to join the revolution! – Enabling new modes of production in the contemporary Danish food system   66
   Martin Hvarregaard Thorsøe, Chris Kjeldsen and Egon Noe

6. Storytelling and meal experience concepts   84
   Lena Mossberg and Dorthe Eide

7. The reinvention of terroir in Danish food place promotion   100
   Szilvia Gyimóthy

Index   117

Citation Information

The chapters in this book were originally published in *European Planning Studies*, volume 25, issue 7 (July 2017). When citing this material, please use the original page numbering for each article, as follows:

Guest Editorial
Emerging Nordic food approaches
Jesper Manniche and Bjørnar Sæther
European Planning Studies, volume 25, issue 7 (July 2017), pp. 1101–1110

Chapter 1
Quality turns in Nordic food: a comparative analysis of specialty food in Denmark, Norway and Sweden
Henrik Halkier, Laura James and Egil Petter Stræte
European Planning Studies, volume 25, issue 7 (July 2017), pp. 1111–1128

Chapter 2
Sustainability transformations in the balance: exploring Swedish initiatives challenging the corporate food regime
Jacob von Oelreich and Rebecka Milestad
European Planning Studies, volume 25, issue 7 (July 2017), pp. 1129–1146

Chapter 4
How relationships can influence an organic firm's network identity
Gunn-Turid Kvam, Hilde Bjørkhaug and Ann-Charlott Pedersen
European Planning Studies, volume 25, issue 7 (July 2017), pp. 1147–1165

Chapter 5
It's never too late to join the revolution! – Enabling new modes of production in the contemporary Danish food system
Martin Hvarregaard Thorsøe, Chris Kjeldsen and Egon Noe
European Planning Studies, volume 25, issue 7 (July 2017), pp. 1166–1183

Chapter 6
Storytelling and meal experience concepts
Lena Mossberg and Dorthe Eide
European Planning Studies, volume 25, issue 7 (July 2017), pp. 1184–1199

Chapter 7
The reinvention of terroir in Danish food place promotion
Szilvia Gyimóthy
European Planning Studies, volume 25, issue 7 (July 2017), pp. 1200–1216

For any permission-related enquiries please visit:
http://www.tandfonline.com/page/help/permissions

Notes on Contributors

Hilde Bjørkhaug is Research Professor in Sociology at the Centre for Rural Research, Universitetssenteret Dragvoll, Trondheim, Norway.

Dorthe Eide works at the Nord University Business School, Bodø, Norway.

Szilvia Gyimóthy is Associate Professor at the Department of Culture and Global Studies, Aalborg University, Copenhagen, Denmark.

Henrik Halkier is Dean of the Department of Culture and Global Studies, Aalborg University, Aalborg, Denmark.

Laura James is Associate Professor at the Department of Culture and Global Studies, Aalborg University, Aalborg, Denmark.

Chris Kjeldsen is Senior Researcher at the Department of Agroecology, Aarhus University, Tjele, Denmark.

Gunn-Turid Kvam is Senior Research at the Centre for Rural Research, Universitetssenteret Dragvoll, Trondheim, Norway.

Jesper Manniche is a Senior Research Fellow experienced within a range of research fields related to rural development including local food networks, innovation and knowledge creation, small businesses and entrepreneurship, and regional governance and policy.

Rebecka Milestad is based at the Department of Sustainable Development, Environmental Sciences and Engineering (SEED), Division of Environmental Strategies Research – fms, KTH Royal Institute of Technology, Stockholm, Sweden.

Lena Mossberg is Professor at the School of Business, Economics and Law, University of Gothenburg, Gothenburg, Sweden.

Egon Noe is Professor and Leader of the Danish Centre for Rural Research, University of Southern Denmark, Esbjerg, Denmark.

Ann-Charlott Pedersen is Professor at the Department of Industrial Economics and Technology Management, NTNU, Trondheim, Norway.

Bjørnar Sæther is Professor of Human Geography with a specialization in economic geography. His teaching and research activities are related to resource based industries, innovation in rural areas and sustainability issues.

Egil Petter Stræte is Senior Researcher at the Centre for Rural Research, Trondheim, Norway.

NOTES ON CONTRIBUTORS

Martin Hvarregaard Thorsøe is a Postdoctoral Researcher at the Department of Agroecology, Aarhus University, Tjele, Denmark.

Jacob von Oelreich is based at the Department of Sustainable Development, Environmental Sciences and Engineering (SEED), Division of Environmental Strategies Research – fms, KTH Royal Institute of Technology, Stockholm, Sweden.

INTRODUCTION

Emerging Nordic food approaches

Jesper Manniche and Bjørnar Sæther

Introduction

This special issue consists of six articles discussing the ongoing changes of food production and consumption in the Nordic countries and in particular the Scandinavian countries of Denmark, Norway and Sweden. The transformation of food production and consumption systems and the social and corporate responses to the observed negative environmental, health and other side-effects of the mainstream, industrialized food production–consumption model have been studied extensively. Research debates have centred around whether and in which ways the emerging new food economy entails a genuine paradigmatic change towards 'post-productivism' (Goodman, 2003; Marsden, 2013; Roche & Argent, 2015) and a 're-territorialization' of the food economy with new opportunities for endogenous sustainable rural development (van der Ploeg & Renting, 2004; Watts, Ilbery, & Maye, 2005; Winter, 2003). Such concerns have been summarized in the notion 'the new rural development paradigm' (Murdoch, 2000). Core conceptualizations of transformations of food systems have been and still are, as documented in the papers included in this special issue; 'conventions of quality' (Storper & Salais, 1997), 'alternative food networks' (Renting, Marsden, & Banks, 2003; Watts et al., 2005), 'short food supply chains' (Marsden, Banks, & Bristow, 2000) and territorially embedded marketing and certification schemes (Ilbery, Morris, Buller, Maye, & Kneafsey, 2005; Parrott, Wilson, & Murdoch, 2002).

Literatures on the emerging new food economy have been dominated by reports from a limited number of countries, in particular the U.K., Holland, Italy and the U.S., while the ongoing changes in the Nordic countries are less comprehensively studied, although they are by no means un-explored (Amilien, Fort, & Ferras, 2007; Byrkjeflot, Pedersen, & Svejenova, 2013). As reported in this special issue, Scandinavian producers, consumers and policy-makers have come quite some way in transforming the approaches to the production and marketing of food. The main part of this transformation parallels with the rest of Europe, however other aspects are uniquely Nordic. From a position with no distinct gastronomic profile, a new internationally trendsetting gourmet restaurant sector has sprung up in since the early 2000s, attracting the attention of global media, gastronomic chefs and 'foodies'. Commentators credit the key initiating and inspirational role for this development to a group of charismatic chefs and gastronomic entrepreneurs, who in 2004 formulated and launched the 'New Nordic Cuisine' (NNC) manifesto. The manifesto aimed for a new way of cooking based on 'ingredients and produce whose characteristics are particularly excellent in our climates, landscapes and waters'.[1] Purity, freshness and seasonality were other salute words in the manifesto. At present, the NNC is one of the most prestigious and internationally successful cooking trends, represented at Bocuse d'Or, the unofficial world championship in cooking, winning in 2009 (Geir Skeie, Norway), 2011 (Rasmus Kofoed, Denmark) and 2015 (Ørjan Johannessen, Norway). Moreover, 11 of the latest 15 winners of gold, silver and bronze medals at the five competitions since 2009 are from Scandinavia.[2] The Copenhagen Restaurant, NoMa, the winner of the British Restaurant Magazine's prize as the world's best restaurant 2010–2012 and again 2014, has been one of the lighthouses of NNC in the shaping of a new Nordic, Scandinavian and Danish food identity and profile.

Notwithstanding the inspirational top-down effects of the NNC manifest and its founding protagonists, the changes of Nordic food markets started decades earlier in the form of pioneering and persistent bottom-up activities of business entrepreneurs and local communities throughout the Nordic countries. From a starting point in the 1980s when markets were utterly dominated by standardized, industrial food, a varied supply of specialized local culinary products has been developed and marketed. Local producer and distributor networks have been established, often as part of territorialized rural development strategies for economic diversification. The new culinary offerings and producer networks have become identity markers and components in place-branding activities of rural and urban tourism destinations and an inspirational basis for attempts at re-inventing regional 'terroir' qualities of food in Scandinavia.

Food transition

Authors in this special issue have been invited due to their differing thematic, theoretical and methodological backgrounds in order to reflect the variety of research communities interested in the topic of food. Thus, the papers apply a range of theoretical and conceptual perspectives such as 'convention theory', 'industrial marketing and purchasing network theory' and 'storytelling in provision of meal experiences'. However, despite the varying thematic and theoretical frameworks, all papers somehow directly or indirectly relate to and add to our knowledge of an ongoing, but far from completed 'transition' of food systems in Scandinavia. Throughout the processes of editing and reviewing the papers, authors have been urged to discuss theoretical and empirical findings in terms of implications for a system-level transition.

During the last 15 years, transition studies have grown considerably in importance, based on early works by Dutch historians and social scientists (e.g. Geels, 2002; Geels & Schot, 2007). Originally, combining insights from economic history, organizational sciences and sociology of technology studies, transition studies have evolved into a framework for analysis of possible sustainable transitions in particular sectors such as energy or transportation. More recently, food has emerged as a sector of interest to transition research (Marsden, 2013; Spaargaren, Oosterveer, & Loeber, 2012).

According to Terry Marsden;

> Transitions may be viewed temporally as periods in which opportunity for change opens up within a system (i.e. a socio-technical regime made up of dominant economic, industrial, political and scientific rules and assumptions) to produce something disconnected to earlier supporting structures, as the dominant system struggles to respond to surrounding (landscape) pressures. (Marsden, 2013, p. 124)

In line with this, transition theories include three interacting societal levels; niches which are the nexus for innovations and new technologies, and the socio-technical regime including the dominating technologies, practices and policies, which determine a certain field of social activity. The third level is the socio-technical landscape which is the exogenous context including cultures changing only slowly.

The temporal dimension is explicit in transition studies, but authors underline the often rather weak spatial perspectives (Coenen, Benneworth, & Truffer, 2012). The lack of spatial perspectives is not, however, a general characteristic of research on food transition, which often suffers from a too strong focus on one particular spatial scale, the local, and thus is caught in what Born and Purcell (2006) term 'the local trap', i.e.

> the tendency of food activists and researchers to assume something inherent about the local scale. The local is assumed to be desirable; it is preferred a priori to larger scales. What is desired varies and can include ecological sustainability, social justice, democracy, better nutrition, and food security, freshness, and quality. (Born & Purcell, 2006, p. 195)

To Born and Purcell, and in the relational transition theory approach of Coenen and colleagues, scale is nothing that exists a priori, but is actively constructed by actors pursuing their goals; 'Actors construct scales as they seek to look after their own interests within the networks most salient to them' (Coenen et al., 2012, p. 975). Actors operating across different scales and places actively construct networks in a process of inter-localization.

Although only few of the articles in this issue explicitly apply transition theory perspectives, they commonly illustrate the possibilities of and obstacles for transitions in differing Scandinavian, national, regional and local contexts as well as the close interaction between the spatial and temporal dimensions of food transitions. A re-occurring challenge for niche producers is how to grow without losing the values – or changing the 'conventions of quality' – that are intimately connected to being supplier of 'organic', 'local' or other food qualities and that are sustained by complex network configurations and negotiations involving varying types of stakeholders. To grow often means re-scaling a firm's operation to reach out to a larger market, i.e. from a local to a national market. Papers in this issue investigate the re-scaling of food business activities in varying territorial and industrial settings, including the altering of relations to actors at other scales, or actors belonging to industrial configurations with other – sometimes conflicting – quality conventions.

Overall changes of food markets

The first paper provides an overall picture of the development of markets for specialty food and drinks in Denmark, Norway and Sweden during recent decades. Henrik Halkier, Laura James and Egil Petter Stræte start with presenting a definition of specialty food including two dimensions; localization and specialization. They go on by comparing, mainly in quantitative terms, the ongoing changes in food production and consumption and the related policies and institutional settings in the three Scandinavian countries. Based on their definition and sets of indicators they find that specialty food has increased in all three countries since the 1990s. Speciality food and drink seem to have a strong position in Sweden, particularly in organic food. Organic farmland represents 15% of total farmland according to the statistics. The figures are 6% and 7% in Norway and Denmark, respectively. Norway has a relatively high number of products protected under labels based on criteria such as taste and raw materials. Denmark has made most use of the New Nordic concept and has seen a remarkable growth in microbreweries.

Halkier and colleagues raise the question to what extent it is possible to outline a 'Scandinavian model' of food governance. They argue that commonalities exist, particularly when it comes to a pattern of extensive interaction between central government, local government and private firms. The emergence of this pattern of interaction can be placed within a distinct historical-geographical context. What we today consider a consolidated niche of organic food has been well under way for decades. For instance, as part of the emergence of the alternative movement in Denmark, organic food was set on the agenda in the 1970s. A few farmers, processors and distributors supplied a minority of consumers, but the policy support and institutional set-up of organic food in Denmark (including a national certification scheme) was starting to emerge already in the 1970s. In the remote valleys of Norway productivist agriculture influenced, but never transformed production or consumption completely. Due to harsh climate and poor soils, large-scale industrialized agriculture as in Denmark and southern Sweden was impossible. Combined with a protectionist agricultural policy, which made imported food rather expensive, local food traditions had a better chance to survive. Thus, producers of specialty products such as fermented trout, beer and cheese were well positioned when urban consumers discovered specialty food from the 1990s and onward. Today several of these producers have obtained national Protected Geographical Indications, based on their ability to innovate from old recipes. Remoteness and an agricultural policy both protectionist and supportive are thus a background for the relative success of specialty food in Norway.

Niches, firms and markets

Three articles deal with food transition from the perspective of niches, product categories and firms, and investigate the implications of systemic change and new market conventions for producers and the networks in which they are part. Based on a critical understanding of the current corporate food regime, Jacob von Oelreich and Rebecka Milestad explore how two Swedish organic initiatives possibly can challenge this regime. Their discussion is based on a distinction between mainstream organic food and an emerging organic 3.0 challenging the mainstream. Organic 3.0 aims for a new level of sustainability, with a stronger focus on systemic impacts including health, ecology, fairness and trade. A distinction between reformist strategies facilitating niche growth and more radical 3.0 approaches that are likely to challenge the regime is introduced. The firm based on mainstreaming has succeeded in supplying large volumes of organic meat to its retail partners. However, the firm had to compromise its identity and the ambition to create a 3.0 niche within the organic niche is by and large unaccomplished. The other firm, an organic box scheme, has been more successful in promoting organic 3.0 values along with its distribution of organic food. It seems however, that keeping to values of fairness and ecology has curbed the growth of the firm.

Gunn-Turid Kvam, Hilde Bjørkhaug and Ann-Charlott Pedersen investigate how changes in network relations can influence an organic firm's identity. Like von Oelreich and Milestad, Kvam and colleagues are concerned about the identity of organic firms, in this case an organic dairy starting to cooperate with a major retailer. The ambition of the mid-scale dairy is to retain its core values while growing into a national supplier through establishing business relations with one of the three major retailers in Norway. The industrial marketing and purchasing perspective guides the analysis of network relationships. Authors point out there are few cases of successful growth strategies among Norwegian mid-scale values based organic firms, the case reported on here might be the only one. The study documents the possibility of staying true to organic values while re-scaling operations from a regional to a national supplier of organic milk.

In the article by Martin Hvarregaard Thorsøe, Chris Kjeldsen and Egon Noe the scale of analysis is shifted from the micro to the meso level, more specific to the product categories craft beer, specialty flour and organic broilers. Their analysis is guided by conventions theory where conventions are seen as an organizing element of actors along the food chain. The case studies demonstrate that if transitions within product categories are to occur, changes have to take place in several domains along the value chain. What the authors term a multidimensional reconfiguration has taken place in the cases of specialty flour and craft beer, but not in the case of organic broilers. Food trends are potentials for change that may or may not find a concrete expression in particular products, dependent on whether quality conventions are interpreted in a way that makes coordinated change possible.

These three papers add knowledge concerning preconditions for successful food transitions and the interdependent re-scaling. Strong organic values and good skills in managing network relations are part of the reason why the mid-scale values based organic diary in Norway succeeded. The two organic Swedish firms experienced success that is more modest and there seems to have been a trade-off between growth and organic values, in particular the 'deeper' organic 3.0 values. The three Danish cases document diversity among transitions of national value chains. The authors emphasize the role of quality conventions, but in their description of why organic broilers so far have not succeeded, material aspects of this particular food commodity, impacting technologies at the abattoirs, are taken into account. Abattoir technological systems are based on economies of scale and are not very flexible for variations in the dimensions of the processed animals. Small batches of organic broilers of varying sizes do not add to the bottom line. In the case of craft beer economies of scale so far have been irrelevant, since consumers are willing to pay a higher price for craft beer. However, this situation may change as the competition among the many new micro breweries is supposed to grow and some breweries will be forced to introduce economics of scale in order to survive in the marketplace.

A lesson learned from these micro- and meso-level case studies is that there is no one way to a transition of individual products or product categories. Food trends, such as the heightened interest in specialty food in general and Nordic food in particular, help establish an action space that may or may not lead to transitions of particular products or product categories in a particular market. However, it is important to stress that what is 'specialized' and what is 'standardized' depends on the temporal and spatial context. In a transition theory perspective, standardization of newly developed 'specialized' products and technologies, upscaling of niche productions and diffusion of the now 'standard' technologies and products are crucial elements in the definition of when transition is achieved and realized. In this sense, a food transition has not been accomplished until former specialized, restricted technologies have become standard and cheaper. As exclusiveness and distinctiveness are important goals for producers and consumers of quality food, this might actually constitute a structural market barrier for fully accomplishing a transition of our food systems. Such a large-scale transition would imply that both producers and consumers would lose precisely what constitute them – their exclusiveness.

To the extent that the articles deal with transition of food systems, they focus on social, cultural and economic aspects and drivers of food transition rather than on environmental aspect. The discussions in the papers are not whether the studied food approaches are more sustainable and environmentally friendly than the dominating food models. Instead, the papers investigate topics such as socially just trade and work relations, consumer experiences and arousing forms of place-branding. This reflects the interests of the contributing authors, but also seems to mirror a more general characteristic of the emerging food approaches in Scandinavia. Regrettably, consumers' concerns for environmental sustainability seem to be subordinate to concerns for individual freedom, feelings against social and economic inequality and individualized preferences.

Food as a means for innovation in tourism and rural development

In the last two articles, the focus is lifted from exploring changes and innovations inside the traditional agri-food sector of farmers, manufacturers and distributors to the investigation of food as a means for tourism innovation, place-branding and economic restructuring of rural areas. The chosen topics of the two papers, storytelling in meal provision and food-based place promotion of rural areas, in themselves are indications that the social and economic landscape for food production and consumption in Scandinavian countries has changed during recent years and new commodification strategies have consolidated. Consumption, including the processes of selecting, purchasing, preparing, consuming, evaluating and memorizing specific goods, is an important part of identity formation and social positioning of individuals and groups (Arnould & Thomson, 2005; Lash & Urry, 1994; Miele, 2006). In transition theory terms, this is an indicator of changes at the landscape level of the present food regime.

The food and drinks sector is an excellent example of such macro trends, inciting innovations at niche and regime levels. The majority of consumers may still consider foods and drinks mainly as tangible goods serving functional purposes (hunger and nutrition) as indicated by the analysis of. Measured in statistical, quantitative terms the industrial food regime may seem only marginally impacted by the introduction of varying types of 'alternative' products in terms of economic structures, power relations and carbon dependency. However, we should not overlook the implications for both small and large producers and retailers of the fact that for a growing minority of consumers food has become a cultural identity marker, loaded with a variety of symbolism and meanings. Storytelling and dialogue with consumers and other stakeholders through packaging, the internet and other channels are today imperative for actors along the supply chain. Furthermore, as evidenced by the two last papers, the creation of supplies of food with a local and regional profile and the establishment of an internationally trendsetting gastronomic sector have provided opportunities for new tourism products and changed the identity and self-promotion strategies of many rural areas.

In their analysis of restaurants and caterers serving tourists, Lena Mossberg and Dorthe Eide retain a basic production-side perspective. However, their theoretical approach differs from most agri-food studies as they apply the 'Experience Economy' (Pine & Gilmore,

1999) as an overall analytic framework for understanding value creation and strategic management of restaurants and tourist attractions. Through three case studies from Sweden and Norway, Mossberg and Eide explore how tourism-based restaurants and attractions in practical terms use storytelling for provision of meal experiences for their visitors, and to what extent storytelling contributes to local socio-economic development.

Although the cases all connect to the 'NNC' as they use local food products and emphasize the freshness and seasonality, they are not the usually researched and media-hyped types of up-market, highly specialized and dedicated gourmet restaurants such as NoMa (Leer, 2016; Petruzzelli & Savino, 2012), with appeal mainly for the segment of 'foodies'. On the contrary, the studied cases target a broader segment of consumers, and rely on a limited offer of standardized, unsophisticated menus, based on traditional Nordic recipes and served to a large number of guests. This allows the restaurants to stick to their respective concepts and control the quality of their offerings. Reliance on, on the one hand, scale, standardization and efficiency, and on the other hand the abilities of delivering unique stories and experiences to consumers with dedicated demands may seem contradictory, but reminds us about the usefulness of the World of Production model of Storper and Salais (1997), applied in numerous food studies (e.g. Manniche & Testa, 2010; Morgan, Marsden, & Murdoch, 2006; Murdoch & Miele, 1999; Stræte, 2008). The model outlines four action frameworks for firms of which the standardization–dedication market world encapsulates the balancing of the above contrary demands. More importantly, the case illustrates that standardization of products, technologies and services is an integral phase of any product/technology life cycle, including the specialized markets for 'unique' New Nordic Food.

Tourism-based activities also form the context for Szilvia Gyimóthy's paper. The object of study here is the food-place promotion of rural tourist destinations in Denmark, especially regarding the construction, legitimization and representation of 'terroir' qualities of local food. Hence, food and food sector activities are studied indirectly via an analysis of the rhetorical approaches applied in diverse tourism promotion materials. Despite this analytical 'outsider' perspective, Gyimóthy connects directly to one of the key questions in the issue, namely what characterizes the emerging Nordic approaches to develop, produce and market local, artisanal food as compared to the approaches applied in other parts of the world such as Southern Europe or North America? Gyimóthy asks it the following way: How should we conceptualize Nordic place promotion strategies and terroir constructions? What rhetoric approaches and ideologies position Nordic regions as food places against more established Mediterranean competitors where gastronomic cultures have evolved over centuries?

Gyimóthy's point is the fact that the exploitation of regional gastronomy and culinary heritage in place-branding is a relatively new phenomenon in the Nordic countries, but during the last decade have become widespread among rural tourist destinations. On the basis of a review of literatures on strategies of commodifying food and rural terroir, which are heavily focused on Mediterranean countries, Gyimóthy classifies two different types of narrative commodification strategies, both 'conservationist' and reflecting contexts where terroir stories are nurtured by arguments of longevity and traditions: accreditation and patrimonialization. According to Gyimóthy, none of these are capable of describing the distinct food commodification strategies applied in Scandinavian contexts, as presented in promotion materials. To close this gap she suggests a conceptualization of 'narrative strategies framing touristic terroir' in which the two above conservationist approaches are supplemented with two 'transformational', exoticising and enterprising strategies. Notwithstanding the current success of such terroir constructions, in which the story-motifs of playful and innovative Nordic gastronomic entrepreneurs have replaced the clichés of agricultural traditions and romantic countryside idyll exploited in South Europe, Gyimóthy also warns they may fall into a conformity trap and fail to single out a distinct identity against more established culinary destinations.

Towards a Nordic food transition?

In analysis of comparative developments in Denmark, Sweden and Norway questions concerning a possible Nordic model are frequently raised. The content of such a model is fluid, but often includes discussions on the welfare state, economic policy and women's rights (Engelstad & Hagelund, 2015). In a discussion of Nordic food transformations it is tempting to look for evidence of a Nordic model of food transformation. In their discussion of a Scandinavian model, Halkier et al. open up the possibility of such a model of food governance, distinguished by extensive interaction between central government, local government and private firms to stimulate growth of specialty food. Indeed, government involvement has been visible particularly on the supply side of specialty food since the 1990s, e.g. in relation to organic food, but we are not able to identify anything near a complete Nordic model of food transitions, unique to this part of Europe. The emergence of specialty food probably has been helped by more systemic characteristics of the Nordic countries that have supported innovation in general. According to one commentator this includes

> … a high degree of labour force egalitarianism and engagement over labour relations as well as technical issues; a strong commitment to high levels of welfare provision and expenditure; a pronounced localism in service delivery in otherwise centralized states and a commitment to often quite radical or communitarian forms of social democracy in the political sphere. (Cooke, 2016, p. 192)

We may add to these conditions the widespread public concerns for and policy towards regulation schemes in support of the environment, even though, as mentioned before, the issue of environmental sustainability certainly not always is the main priority of Scandinavian producers and consumers.

These qualities of Nordic societies are however not articulated into any sort of action plan to challenge the current food regime. We consider the current food regime with its major actors including retailers, food processing industry and industrialized agriculture to continue 'business as usual', controlling something like 95% of the market among them. There do not seem to be major cracks in the regime that cannot be adjusted by regime actors themselves. Nevertheless, even though a diminishing number of actors control a growing part of the value chain, the conditions for competing on markets for foods and drinks unquestionably have changed since the 1990s. Even a large transnational corporation like Carlsberg has not been able to control the taste of beers of consumers in its home market. Danish beer drinkers have demonstrated that they are willing to pay more for craft beer and that economy of scale is not always the most profitable strategy for producers. The case of Danish craft beer and several other cases discussed in this special issue warn researchers that figures of market shares among the big processors and retailers only tells a part of the picture. Even the largest retailers have had to make adjustments to allow small, local or organic producers to offer their products in their stores. These examples clearly illustrate that the lines between what once were two distinct supply chains, the conventional and the alternative, have become occluded and no longer should be considered in dichotomist terms (Sonnino & Marsden, 2006).

The articles in this special issue explore how these lines have become blurred but surely do not present the concluding answers. The editors propose comparative research across Europe to learn more about the regional differences in what seems to be an omnipresent but slowly emerging food transition. Such research should include efforts to establish better, and publicly available, quantitative data on this transition. While there is a lot of interest in questions concerning possible transformations in sectors such as energy and transportation, no issue or 'sector' is actually more encompassing than the food we eat. Ludwig Andreas Feuerbach formulated this quite eloquently already in 1863; 'Der Mensch ist, was er ißt.'

Notes

1. See http://www.clausmeyer.dk/en/the_new_nordic_cuisine_.html.
2. The Bocuse d'Or Winners' Academy, 2016, http://www.bocusedor-winners.com/uk/chefs/.

Disclosure statement

No potential conflict of interest was reported by the authors.

References

Amilien, V., Fort, F., & Ferras, N. (2007, March). Hyper-real territories and urban markets: Changing conventions for local food – case studies from France and Norway. *Anthropology of Food*. Retrieved from http://aof.revues.org/446

Arnould, E. J., & Thomson, C. J. (2005). Reflections. Consumer culture theory (CCT): Twenty years of research. *Journal of Consumer Research*, 31, 868–882. doi:10.1086/426626

Born, B., & Purcell, M. (2006). Avoiding the local trap. Scale and food systems in planning research. *Journal of Planning Education and Research*, 26, 195–207. doi:10.1177/0739456X06291389

Byrkjeflot, H., Pedersen, J. S., & Svejenova, S. (2013). From label to practice: The process of creating new Nordic cuisine. *Journal of Culinary Science & Technology*, 11(1), 36–55. doi:10.1080/15428052.2013.754296

Coenen, L., Benneworth, P., & Truffer, B. (2012). Toward a spatial perspective on sustainability transitions. *Research Policy*, 41, 968–979. doi:10.1016/j.respol.2012.02.014

Cooke, P. (2016). Nordic innovation models: Why is Norway different? *Norwegian Journal of Geography*, 70, 190–201. doi:10.1080/00291951.2016.1167120

Engelstad, F., & Hagelund, A. (2015). *Cooperation and conflict the Nordic way: Work, welfare, and institutional change in Scandinavia*. Berlin: De Gruyter Open.

Geels, F. (2002). Technological transitions as evolutionary reconfiguration processes: A multi-level perspective and a case-study. *Research Policy*, 31(8/9), 1257–1274. doi:10.1016/S0048-7333 (02)00062-8

Geels, F. W., & Schot, J. (2007). Typology of sociotechnical transition pathways. *Research Policy*, 36, 399–417. doi:10.1016/j.respol.2007.01.003

Goodman, D. (2003). Editorial. The quality 'turn' and alternative food practices: Reflections and agenda. *Journal of Rural Studies*, 19, 1–7. doi:10.1016/S0743-0167(02)00043-8

Ilbery, B., Morris, C., Buller, H., Maye, D., & Kneafsey, M. (2005). Product, process and place. An examination of food marketing and labelling schemes in Europe and North America. *European Urban and Regional Studies, 12*(2), 116–132. doi:10.1177/0969776405048499

Lash, S., & Urry, J. (1994). *Economies of signs & space*. London: Sage.

Leer, J. (2016). The rise and fall of the new Nordic cuisine. *Journal of Aesthetics & Culture, 8*(1), doi:10.3402/jac.v8.33494

Manniche, J., & Testa, S. (2010). Knowledge bases in worlds of production: The case of the food industry. *Industry and Innovation, 17*(3), 263–284. doi:10.1080/13662711003790627

Marsden, T. (2013). From post-productionism to reflexive governance: Contested transitions in securing more sustainable food futures. *Journal of Rural Studies, 29*, 123–134. doi:10.1016/j.jrurstud.2011.10.001

Marsden, T., Banks, J., & Bristow, G. (2000). Food supply chain approaches: Exploring their role in rural development. *Sociologia Ruralis, 40*(4), 424–438. doi:10.1111/1467-9523.00158

Miele, M. (2006). Consumption culture: The case of food. In P. Cloke, T. Marsden, & P. Mooney (Eds.), *The handbook of rural studies* (pp. 345–355). Thousand Oaks, CA: Sage.

Morgan, K., Marsden, T., & Murdoch, J. (2006). *Worlds of food: Place, power, and provenance in the food chain*. Oxford: Oxford University Press.

Murdoch, J. (2000). Networks – a new paradigm of rural development? *Journal of Rural Studies, 16*, 407–419. doi:10.1016/S0743-0167(00)00022-X

Murdoch, J., & Miele, M. (1999). 'Back to nature': Changing 'worlds of production' in the food sector. *Sociologia Ruralis, 39*(4), 465. doi:10.1111/1467-9523.00119

Parrott, N., Wilson, N., & Murdoch, J. (2002). Spatializing quality: Regional protection and the alternative geography of food. *European Urban and Regional Studies, 9*(3), 241–261. doi:10.1177/096977640200900304

Petruzzelli, A. M., & Savino, T. (2012). Search, recombination, and innovation: Lessons from haute cuisine. *Long Range Planning*. doi.org/10.1016/j.lrp.2012.09.001

Pine, B. J., & Gilmore, J. H. (1999). *The experience economy: Work is theatre and every business a stage*. Boston, MA: Harvard Business School Press.

Renting, H., Marsden, T., & Banks, J. (2003). Understanding alternative food networks: Exploring the role of short food supply chains in rural development. *Environment and Planning A, 35*(3), 393–411. doi:10.1068/a3510

Roche, M., & Argent, N. (2015). The fall and rise of the agricultural productivism? An antipodean viewpoint. *Progress in Human Geography, 39*(5), 621–635. doi:10.1177/0309132515582058

Sonnino, R., & Marsden, T. (2006). Beyond the divide: Rethinking relationships between alternative and conventional food networks in Europe. *Journal of Economic Geography, 6*, 181–199. doi:10.1093/jeg/lbi006

Spaargaren, G., Oosterveer, P., & Loeber, A. (2012). Sustainability transitions in food consumption, retail and production. In G. Spaargaren, P. Oosterveer, & A. Loeber (Eds.), *Food practices in transition. Changing food consumption, retail and production in the age of reflexive modernity* (pp. 1–34). New York, NY: Routledge.

Storper, M., & Salais, R. (1997). *Worlds of production: The action frameworks of the economy*. Boston, MA: Harvard University Press.

Stræte, E. P. (2008). Modes of qualities in development of specialty food. *British Food Journal, 110*(1), 62–75. doi:10.1108/00070700810844795

van der Ploeg, J. D., & Renting, H. (2004). Behind the 'Redux': A rejoinder to David Goodman. *Sociologia Ruralis, 44*(2), 233–242. doi:10.1111/j.1467-9523.2004.00272.x

Watts, D. C. H., Ilbery, B., & Maye, D. (2005). Making reconnections in agro-food geography: Alternative systems of food provision. *Progress in Human Geography, 29*(1), 22–40. doi:10.1191/0309132505ph526oa

Winter, M. (2003). Geographies of food: Agro-food geographies – making reconnections. *Progress in Human Geography, 27*(4), 505–513. doi:10.1191/0309132503ph446pr

Quality turns in Nordic food: a comparative analysis of specialty food in Denmark, Norway and Sweden

Henrik Halkier, Laura James and Egil Petter Stræte

ABSTRACT
This article compares the development of specialty food in Denmark, Norway and Sweden using a number of quantitative indicators as well as a qualitative analysis of government policy. The analysis shows that specialty food has increased in importance in all three countries over the last twenty years, but there are important differences in the kind of specialty food that has developed and the nature of government intervention and governance structures. Overall, Sweden appears to have the largest production of specialty food and drink and is particularly strong in organic production and consumption, farm processing and farm shops. Norway has a large number of products with protected origin and also leads in the number of farmers' markets. Denmark lags behind the other countries on most indicators, but has witnessed the fastest growth in microbreweries over the last five years. Theoretically, the article challenges the 'negative' definition of specialty food as 'non-industrial' or 'alternative', and suggests a more nuanced approach. Empirically, it points towards the possible existence of a 'Scandinavian model' of specialty food governance with extensive interaction between central government, local government and private firms to stimulate the growth of specialty food.

1. Introduction

Specialty food has qualities related to the origin of production or processing methods that differentiate it significantly from industrial, mass-produced, conventional food. It is part of a wider international trend, which has been termed the 'quality turn' (Murdoch, Marsden, & Banks, 2000). In Scandinavia, specialty food has become associated with the New Nordic food concept which was introduced in 2004 by 12 Nordic chefs who wrote a manifesto emphasizing the value of authentic regional cooking and the importance of organic produce (Nordic Council, 2015). By comparing the development and governance of specialty food in three Scandinavian countries, this article aims to make two contributions to the existing academic literature. First, from a theoretical perspective, the article helps to refine the essentially 'negative' definition of specialty food as 'non-industrial' (Stræte, 2016) or 'alternative' (Tregear, 2011), and instead calls for a more nuanced approach to the study of emerging forms of food, including the New Nordic trend. Secondly, it presents empirical evidence that despite variations in the development of different types of specialty food, a Scandinavian model seems to exist.

The text is divided in three parts. Firstly, a conceptual framework is outlined on the basis of existing contributions to the literature on specialty food, including issues related to governance. Then an attempt is made to gauge the extent to which different forms of specialty food have come to prominence in Denmark, Norway and Sweden. Finally, the governance structures for specialty food in the three countries are compared.

2. Conceptual framing of specialty food

The notion of 'specialty food' is related to other concepts such as 'alternative food' (Renting, Marsden, & Banks, 2003; Tregear, 2011) and 'quality food' (Goodman, 2003; Kjeldsen, Deleuran, & Noe, 2013; Murdoch et al., 2000) in the sense that they all focus on what they are not, namely standardized industrial products aimed at mass markets in which price is the main competitive parameter. It is, of course, widely acknowledged that these 'negative' or inverted categories are relational and symbolic constructs that are highly context-dependent (Testa, 2011). For the purpose of conducting a comparative study, the notion of specialty food is particularly helpful, because attempts have been made to systematically distinguish between types of non-industrial qualities (Stræte, 2016). While some forms of specialty food consumption are primarily defined by their intended impact on consumers (e.g. in terms of health or pleasure/experience) (Manniche & Larsen, 2013; Roininen, Arvola, & Lähteenmäki, 2006), this article focuses on two supply-side dimensions that have also been routinely associated with 'alternative' or 'quality' food (e.g. Hegnes, 2013; Kvam, Magnus, & Stræte, 2014; Morris & Young, 2000; O'Reilly & Haines, 2004; Storstad, 2008; Stræte, 2008); namely, food that is (1) local in the sense of being sold with reference to its geographical origin or close to its place of production, and (2) produced or processed differently from conventional industrial food, for example, organic or small scale.

Market demand is an important driver of specialty food, with consumers emphasizing issues such as health, the environment, supporting local communities or searching for personal experience (Feldmann & Hamm, 2015; Therkelsen & Blichfeldt, 2012). From this perspective, the appeal of New Nordic food draws on several consumer trends and existing studies (e.g. Micheelsen, Holm, & Jensen, 2013) not only confirm the broad appeal of this form of food, but also indicate that it has a somewhat 'elitist' social bias. Conversely, research on supply-side drivers has focused on the local/organic/small-scale food producer as an entrepreneur and the skills and capabilities that are required to establish and expand new specialty food firms (Coenen & Moodysson, 2009; Kjeldsen et al., 2013; Kvam et al., 2014; Thorsøe et al., in press; Vik & McElwee, 2011). There is also interest in the knowledge processes involved in switching from conventional to specialty food (Eriksen & Sundbo, 2015; Manniche & Larsen, 2013). However, the existing literature on local/organic/small-scale food is characterized by a focus on particular national or regional contexts, and specific types of specialty food production. Thus, there is a need for broader comparative perspectives. This is particularly relevant in a Scandinavian context where, despite general political similarities and a shared cooperative tradition in agri-food/retailing, the national innovation systems differ with regard to the prominence of small firms (less pronounced in Denmark) and the role of the science–technology–innovation paradigm (more prominent in Sweden) (Cooke, 2016).

Demand and supply drivers are influenced by public initiatives to stimulate and support the development of specialty food as well as wider patterns of social interaction between public and private actors. The difference between the Scandinavian welfare societies and market-oriented Anglo-Saxon or statist continental European ones was highlighted in Esping-Andersen's classic *Three worlds of welfare capitalism* (1990). Scandinavia's image as being more equitable, decentralized, green and high-tech efficient seems to linger on (Cox, 2004; Ingebritsen, 2002). While governance in Scandinavia has been affected by the rise of neo-liberal politics (Wiborg, 2013), public welfare policies are still important in many areas related to specialty food such as sustainable development, rural development or consumer satisfaction, involving, for example:

- *certification of products* on the basis of origin and production methods (Parrott, Wilson, & Murdoch, 2002);
- *public procurement* that creates a market for, for example, local or organic food (He & Mikkelsen, 2014);
- *mobilization and competence development* of producers and processors to increase the supply (Daugbjerg & Svendsen, 2010);
- *network creation* between producers in order to facilitate mutual support and joint promotional activities (James & Halkier, 2014; Vitterso & Jervell, 2011);
- *public promotion* towards local consumers or potential visitors (Byrkjeflot, Pedersen, & Svejenova, 2013; Hegnes, 2015).

These forms of direct government intervention to promote the production and consumption of specialty food can be found throughout Europe and beyond (Marsden & Smith, 2005; Parrott et al., 2002), but the relative balance between them may help to shape distinct development paths for forms of specialty food in Scandinavian countries. This might set these countries apart from both the market-lead Anglo-Saxon experience and the more statist approach (Goodman, 2003; cf. Che, Week, & Veeck, 2005; Parrott et al., 2002). The comparative design of the research reported here reflects these theoretical concerns.

2.1. Methodological issues

The international comparative analysis of specialty food in Denmark, Norway and Sweden presented in this article is based on academic and policy studies, statistics, the Internet and media. We have, as far as possible, conducted a systematic comparison using comparable statistical data from Eurostat in order to minimize problems related to the different definitions of variables and/or collection of data in the three countries (Hantrais, 2009). A key issue is the delimitation of specialty food. This sector is rather new and international standards for statistics are not established. We have chosen indicators that cover the two main dimensions of specialty food we identified earlier, and hence, unlike, for example, Thorsøe et al. (in press), the article does not explore in detail the differences between individual specialty products. The prevalence of localized food is indicated through the achievement of protected destination of origin labels, the number of enterprises engaged in farm processing and sale of local food, as well the number of farmers' markets. Proxies for specialized production or processing methods are organic food production and sales, and the development of microbreweries, which is an indicator of small-scale production and/or craft techniques.

3. Specialty food in Denmark, Norway and Sweden

Denmark and the Southern part of Sweden have much better climatic conditions for large-scale farming than Norway, and especially for Denmark these advantages have enabled food to be developed to a large export industry. Regarding political institutional framework for the agriculture and food industry, while Denmark has been a member of the European Union (EU) since 1973 and Sweden since 1995, Norway is not part of the EU or the Common Agricultural Policy.

Table 1 shows that turnover and employment in the food and drink industries are highest in Denmark, but Norway has the highest value added. It is notable that there are far fewer companies operating in the food and drink industries in Denmark compared to that in the other two countries: 1575 compared to 2071 in Norway and 3820 in Sweden. This is reflected in the statistics on the size of enterprises in terms of the average number of people employed per enterprise (see Table 2). Denmark has the largest average in both food and drink enterprises, while Sweden has the smallest, with Norway closer to Sweden. The fact that Sweden and Norway have a larger number of micro- and small-sized enterprises suggests that specialty products may be more prevalent in these countries, while industrial mass-produced food products predominate in Denmark.

3.1. Protected regional food labels

In the EU, certain regional and traditional food and drink products are protected with labels which indicate that they 'harness local or regional skills, traditions, resources and/or climatic factors in the production methods ... which have not been protected by

Table 1. Key indicators in food and drink industries (2013).

	Denmark	Sweden	Norway
Turnover (billion €)	24.7	19.6	22.5
Value added (billion €)	4.2	4.2	4.6
Number of employees (1000s)[a]	60.4	54.9	49.7
Number of enterprises	1575	3820	2071

Source: Eurostat: Annual detailed enterprise statistics for industry (NACE Rev. 2, B-E), http://ec.europa.eu/eurostat/data/database.
[a]Part-time employees included.

Table 2. Food and drink industries: average size in number of employed per enterprise (2013).

Number of employed per enterprise						
Denmark		Norway		Sweden	
Food	Drink	Food	Drink	Food	Drink
39.9	36.7	23.6	34.8	16.1	22.0

Source: Eurostat: Annual detailed enterprise statistics for industry (NACE Rev. 2, B-E), http://ec.europa.eu/eurostat/data/database.

trademarks' (Parrott et al., 2002, p. 214). The three EU designations are known as PDO (protected designation of origin), PGI (protected geographical indication) and TSG (traditional speciality guaranteed), and Table 3 illustrates Becker and Staus' (2009, p. 128) point that in Scandinavian countries, 'there are hardly any collective quality marks, a low level of and hardly any growth rate in PDO/PGI registration'. However, Norway has its own version of the EU scheme and, in 2015, 23 products had one of these three protection labels in the national scheme. Moreover, Norway also has another label called *Spesialitet* (Specialty) with criteria related to unique taste, made in Norway, specific raw materials, method of processing and/or a recipe. Under this label, 211 products were certified in February 2016 (Matmerk, 2016c).

3.2. Farm processing and local production

The definition of 'local food' and 'local production' varies not only between countries, but also between different contexts within countries. In some cases, local food is defined on the basis of distance from the producer to the retailer (as is the case for Swedish farmers' markets); in other cases, local food is defined on the basis of a traditional recipe or regional specialty (as in Norway).

In Denmark, national statistics indicate a growing trend for the processing of produce on farms. Between 2007 and 2012, the number of farms engaging in food processing increased from 343 to 631 (Regeringen, 2012), and the number of farm shops also nearly doubled (Thorsøe et al., in press).

In Norway farm processing of food has grown in terms of number of producers and sales volume since its humble beginnings in the early 1990s. The association HANEN (2016) (which organizes activities related to rural tourism and local food) estimates that the number of their members processing farm food has increased from 133 in 2009 to 166 in 2015. The national government hopes to increase the sale of local food to 1 billion Euros in 2025 (Matmerk, 2016b). Local food is here defined as 'food and drink products with local identity or a distinctive origin or especially qualities related to production methods, tradition or product history' (Matmerk, 2016b).

In Sweden the *Lantbrukarnas Riksförbund* (LRF), a membership-based organization for farmers, collates statistics from *Jordbruksverket* (Board of Agriculture) on the production of different foodstuffs and also provides some statistics on local food production and processing based on their membership. Their figures, based on a membership survey from 2013 to 2014, show that the number of firms engaged in local processing was 1002 (up 3.1% from 2011), while the number of farm shops had decreased from 782 to 774 between 2011 and 2013. In their more recently published *Food Strategy for Sweden* (2015), LRF estimates that between 1800 and 2000 companies in Sweden are involved in local food processing. The LRF (2015) noted that one quarter of all municipalities have a goal to increase the proportion of local food they buy and half wanted to increase the proportion of Swedish meat they served in public eateries.

Table 3. PDO, PGI and TSG.

	Denmark	Norway	Sweden
Year first product	1996	2014 (2004)	1997
Products in 2015	6 (PGI)	1 (PGI) (23 in national scheme)	3 (PDO) 3 (PGI) 2 (TSG)

3.3. Farmers' markets

No farmers' market association or organization exists in Denmark, which makes it difficult to estimate the number of regular farmers' markets. The VisitDenmark website notes that farmers' markets and food festivals are rare in Denmark, a fact they attribute to efficient distribution networks. The Organic Association (Økologisk Landsforening) organizes an organic autumn market event every year which involved over 40 farms across Denmark in 2015, and a survey undertaken in spring 2015 identified 82 food-related events throughout the country, some repeated on a weekly basis and others stand-alone/weekend events (Tranholm & Halkier, 2015).

The organization *Bondens Marked* (2016) (farmers' market) in Norway was established in 2003, but they remain a relatively minor distribution channel, even with a record turnover of almost 7 million EUR in 2014. In 2015, markets were regularly open at 34 places in Norway. In addition, there are a number of national and regional festivals related to specialty food and a number of smaller local food-related events.

In Sweden the farmers' market association *Bondens Egen Marknad Riksförening* has 22 market-members and represents 500 rural businesses. The association was established in 2001 and is organized around the concept of local food, which in Sweden is defined as food from farms located within a radius of 250 km of the shop or market where it is sold (reflecting the large distances between settlements in many parts of Sweden). In addition, regional and local food festivals are held across the country.

3.4. Organic products

Organic food is the most prominent form of specialty food in the three countries. Table 4 presents a selection of key statistics about the production and sale of organic products in the three countries. They show that Sweden is more advanced in terms of organic agricultural land, number of organic producers and retail sales of organic food. This is, of course, partly related to the fact that it has the largest land area and population of the three countries. However, it also has more than double the percentage of organic as a percentage of total utilized agricultural land (15%) compared to both Denmark (7%) and Norway (6%).

In Denmark, organic production began to increase after the 1970s where organic agriculture was seen as part of a wider critique of capitalism. Production took off in the mid-1990s when the big supermarket chains started to compete in this niche market. Targeted government subsidies were introduced that supported conversion to organic practices (Ingemann, 2006), based on a national organic certification scheme. Subsidies are still available for farmers who wish to convert to organic agriculture.

In Norway the first organic association was established in 1950 and the certification of organic produce began in the mid-1980s. Subsequently, EU regulations on organic

Table 4. Organic food and drink in Scandinavia (2012).

	Sweden	Denmark	Norway
Organic agricultural land area (hectares)	477,685	182,930	55,260
Organic as % of total utilized agricultural land	15%	7%	6%
Number of organic producers	5601	2677	2590
Number of organic processors	680	517	672
Retail sales (EUR)	917 million	887 million	209 million

Note: Area and operator data: Eurostat, Debio. Market data: SLF; Statistics Sweden, Statistics Denmark; Organic Denmark.

farming were implemented in Norway in 1994 as part of the Agreement on the European Economic Area, and at the same time, a conversion grant was instituted. This conversion grant is being phased out from 2014, but there are other economic supports available for organic productions and projects.

Sweden has a long history of organic farming with the *Biodynamiska Foreningen* (Organic Association) founded in 1940. In the mid-1980s, the KRAV organization was established to develop and promote organic certification of products. Support delivered through the EU structural funds has been available for conversion to organic.

In all three countries, national government has set targets to increase the amount of organic food produced. Sweden had a national target for 20% of agricultural land to be certified organic by 2014 and 25% of food procurement in the public sector to be organic by 2013 (although these targets were not met and the current government is considering whether to set new goals). Denmark has a national action plan on organic food with the objective of doubling the area used for organic farming in Denmark by 2020. There are also goals to increase the amount of organic food served in public institutions, increase exports and introduce new organic products. Norway also has a national target of 15% of food production and 15% consumption to be organic by 2020 (Landbruks- og matdepartementet, 2011).

3.5. Microbreweries and craft beer

The brewing industry in Denmark is dominated by the multinational firm Carlsberg, which has a 63% share of the Danish beer market. However, more independent and small local breweries began to enter the market from the late 1990s, and today Denmark has a thriving specialty beer and microbrewery scene (Thorsøe et al., in press). A new trade organization *Danske Bryghuse* was set up to represent the interests of smaller breweries in 2003, and the growing importance of the specialty beer market is indicated by the establishment of specialty brands by larger players such as Carlsberg.

Norway has restrictive laws regarding the sale of alcohol and a highly concentrated market. Carlsberg/Ringnes and Hansa Borg have a market share of over 80%. Beer stronger than 4.75% alcohol by volume can only be sold in the state monopoly *Vinmonopol*, which traditionally had a very small selection. As in Sweden and Denmark, there has been an upsurge of interest in specialty beers and the establishment of new breweries in recent years. The trade association Bryggeri- og drikkevareforeningen has 71 small-scale breweries as members in 2015. The market share for microbreweries has grown from 0.6% in 2010 to 3.7% in 2015 (Bryggeri- og drikkevareforeningen, 2016).

In Sweden the brewing industry is highly regulated. The state monopoly *Systembolaget* is currently the only outlet allowed to sell spirits, wine and beer stronger than 3.5%. From the 1950s to 1980s, the number of breweries in Sweden declined steadily as a result of the liberalization of competition laws and resulting rationalization. By the early 1990s, there were only seven brewing companies, with Carlsberg controlling over half of the market. However, entry to the EU in 1995 prompted the relaxation of some laws on alcohol sales, and since then, the variety of beer available in Sweden has increased dramatically, as has the number of breweries. Festivals such as the Stockholm Beer Festival (the largest of its kind in Scandinavia) have also raised consumer awareness of, and demand for, craft beers.

Overall, these indicators suggest that the production and consumption of specialty foods take slightly different forms in each of the three countries. In terms of organic

Table 5. Number of microbreweries.

	Sweden	Denmark	Norway
2008	15	N/A	10
2014	149	115	65

Source: The Brewers of Europe (2014, 2015).

food, Sweden has by far the largest area of organic agricultural land, number of producers and processors. All three, however, have national targets to increase the share of organic food. In all three countries, there are very few products registered in the EU regional specialty food product protection schemes, although Norway has its own national scheme with 23 registered products. In terms of farm processing and local food, data from national farming associations indicate that Sweden has the largest number of farm processers, although the numbers have increased in all three countries in recent years. Data on the sale of local food through farmers' markets are similarly patchy. National associations exist in Norway and Sweden and data from these indicate that at least markets are regularly operating in these countries. Finally, the number of microbreweries has increased dramatically in all three countries in recent years, although overall the market for beer is still utterly dominated by the multinational Carlsberg (Table 5).

4. Governance of specialty food development in Denmark, Norway and Sweden

This section analyses the governance of specialty food in the three Scandinavian countries, identifying the similarities and differences between the national settings in terms of aims, methods and institutional set-ups. Starting with a brief outline of the national and European governance of the dominant industrial paradigm in food and drink, the analysis then covers three areas of public policy that could explain the emergence of alternative forms of food and drink, namely, measures targeting:

- producers, for example organic farmers, in order to increase supply;
- consumers, by promoting the importance of special qualities, for example local provenance, in order to increase demand;
- localities and regions, by using, for example, artisanal food production, food as experience and cultural aspects of food as a means to further economic activity in rural areas.

Each of these areas have been subject to public policy for many decades, involving both national and regional/local initiatives, and hence some of the differences between the three countries with regard to specialty food may have been influenced by the different ways in which various policy streams have unfolded and interacted.

4.1. Producing new qualities: policies for organics and beyond

For decades, the aim of agricultural policy in all three countries has been similar; namely, to support efficient mass production of food, either in order to maintain self-sufficiency in basic foodstuffs (Sweden and Norway) or to support agriculture and food production as major export industries (Denmark) (Almås, 2004; LRF, 2015; Manniche, 2010; Manniche & Larsen, 2013). However, alongside the dominant focus on the mass production of food for national and international markets, all three countries have also instituted policies that aim to further the production of specialty food with additional qualities.

In Denmark two types of specialty foods have been in focus, namely, organic produce and local/artisanal food products. Over the last two decades, the government-certified organic sector has been gradually 'integrated in the agro-political and agro-industrial complex' (Ingemann, 2006, p. 43), and the previous centre-left government had ambitious plans for increasing the share of organic food by using public kitchens and landownership to drive change (Regeringen, 2012), although the extent to which this will be pursued by the new right-wing government, in power from 2015, is not yet clear.

The early and relatively successful growth of organic specialty food can be contrasted with the later, and more limited, efforts with regard to 'local food', where public initiatives only became prominent from 2006 onwards, primarily through subnational initiatives funded by either the newly created regions or the local action groups of the European rural development programmes (Danske Regioner, 2011; Henriksen & Halkier, 2015; Manniche, 2008). Here the main policy instrument has been to establish publically subsidized networks between existing producers in order for them to learn from each other and raise their profile vis-à-vis prospective customers (Eriksen & Sundbo, 2015; Jørgensen, Halkier, & James, 2015). While the exposure of, and demand for, local food has certainly increased over the last 10 years, it still has not become part of the mainstream food supply chain.

In Sweden, support for the production of specialty food has also been part of public policy since the mid-1980s when the KRAV certification was instituted (KRAV, 2016). The expansion of sustainable forms of agriculture has been supported through European programmes since Sweden's accession to the EU in 1995 and especially since 2000 where common agricultural policy expanded its less productivist policy activities. As in Denmark, expansion of organic foods has been encouraged through increased production and targets for public procurement (LRF, 2015). In 2007 national government established a six-year programme called *Sverige Matlandet* (Food Country Sweden), and subsequently spent more than 1 billion SEK on encouraging production and consumption of Swedish quality food for the domestic market and international visitors (Jordbruksverket, 2010, 2013). *Matlandet* included support for high-value food with special qualities such as small-scale, organic and local produce, as well as support for innovation in individual firms and networking platforms with a focus on public procurement (Jordbruksverket, 2013; Mat- och Jordbruksnätverket Naturskyddsföreningen, 2012). However, the official evaluation of the programme was reportedly poor (Holmqvist, 2013), and in 2014 the programme was discontinued by the new government, with a new food strategy due to be published in spring 2016 (Dagens Opinion, 2015). This does not, however, imply that local food is currently no longer the subject of public policy. Initiatives continue at the regional level, as will be evident from the discussion below.

In Norway public support for specialty food also goes back decades. The Norwegian government has set 15% as the target for certified organic food production and consumption in 2020 (Landbruks- og matdepartementet, 2011). However, in 2014 the figure was around 5% and the realism of this ambition is in doubt. Interestingly, Norwegian efforts with regard to local food appear to be more successful. In the late 1990s, incentives were established for farm processing, and government initiatives have contributed to the establishment of 900–1000 local food businesses (Bjørkhaug & Kvam, 2011; Kvam & Magnus, 2011). This was followed from 2001 by a 10-year government programme *VSP mat* (Verdiskapingsprogrammet for matproduksjon - programme for value-added food) established in cooperation with the Norwegian farmers' associations with the purpose of creating added value by stimulating the production of food with traditional character and quality. The programme was well-funded (Kjus, Utgård, Pettersen, Svennerud, & Eriksen, 2009), and its main elements were support to firm-based projects including start-ups, networks and competence development, as well as marketing and festivals (Landbruksdepartementet, 2001). An evaluation of the programme concluded that it had a positive impact on diversity of products in the Norwegian food sector (Kjus et al., 2009), and many elements were continued after the end of the programme (Innovasjon Norge, 2016). The Norwegian government has ambitions for further growth of local food, aiming to increase sales from the current 447 million Euros to 1 billion Euros in 2025 (Landbruks- og matdepartementet, 2015), and in early 2016 a new web portal was launched, *Lokalmat* (Local Food), with 272 producers registered when launched (414 by September 2016). Based on collaboration between the business sector, especially the main retailers, and the Norwegian Ministry of Agriculture and Food (Matmerk, 2016a), this new initiative in many ways complements earlier efforts in building a 'food chain' from local producers towards regional/national consumer markets.

4.2. Consumer-oriented information and marketing initiatives

In recent decades, specialty food has also been promoted through public policies supporting the consumption of food with particular qualities through information and marketing.

In addition to the well-established organic certification schemes, all three countries also have some form of spatial certification system in operation, as described in Section 3.2, but compared to especially Mediterranean countries which account for nearly 80% of all EU certifications (calculated on the basis of DG Agriculture, 2016), the limited interest from Danish and Swedish producers reflects the broader north/south divide in Europe with regard to geographical indications as a means to promote specialty food (Parrott et al., 2002; Tregear, Arfini, Belletti, & Marescotti, 2007).

In addition to policies that promote specific products through protective measures, all three countries have also seen initiatives that try to influence consumer preference for specialty food on the basis of their geographical origin by means of branding measures, that is, promotion of the virtues of the produce/products of a particular country/region/locality on the basis of its assumed connection with the territory. Such measures have become widespread in recent decades (Everett & Aitchison, 2008; Gössling & Hall, 2013), but the ways in which these have been brought to bear vary across Scandinavia.

In Denmark, national efforts have concentrated on the health aspects of the New Nordic Diet through a major research project hosted at the University of Copenhagen that has been disseminating its very positive results energetically, despite some public scepticism (Micheelsen et al., 2013). Although the national tourism promotion body, VisitDenmark, has to some extent used food in its efforts to attract international visitors, the presence of quality food on local and regional tourism websites is uneven. The main communication efforts have been undertaken by a large number of networks initiated as part of regional or rural development policy, such as *Smagen af Danmark* and its associated regional/local producer networks. Their aim is to raise the profile of local produce and products primarily with local consumers rather than visitors or a national audience (Therkelsen & Halkier, 2015).

In contrast, Swedish efforts have been prominent at the national level through the *Matlandet* programme. In parallel with this, regional initiatives have been taken in many Swedish regions (Jordbruksverket, 2010, 2016), with some, such as Skåne and Jämtland, succeeding in creating a particularly high profile for themselves (Backe, 2013; Bonow & Rytkönen, 2012). Despite the demise of *Matlandet*, the virtues of Swedish food continue to be promoted through the *Smake Sverige* (Taste Sweden) website of the Swedish Board of Agriculture (Jordbruksverket, 2016).

In Norway, sustained national efforts have concentrated on promoting 'local' quality food since 2001, partly by increasing small-scale production of specialty food as discussed above and partly through promotional efforts in the form of marketing and events (Kjus et al., 2009). This strategy, in addition to identifying Norwegian products with the established label *Nyt Norge* (Enjoy Norway), can be regarded as an attempt to increase the Norwegian food sector's capability of competition by emphasizing the quality dimensions of the products (Hegnes, 2015). Only relatively recently, in 2011, the first regional food manifesto was signed in Trøndelag, based on the New Nordic principles, and, interestingly, the new web *Lokalmat* portal launched in early 2016 with nearly 272 producers registered was clearly 'not' aimed at raising consumer awareness of local food, but was set up as a facilitator of trade between producers, retailers and professional caterers (Matmerk, 2016a).

4.3. Policies for local and regional growth

Policies involving specialty food have been part and parcel of regional and rural development policies in Europe for a couple of decades, for two closely linked reasons. Firstly, many of Europe's lagging regions and localities are rural, hence the quest for viable economic activities through diversification and multifunctional farming (Daugbjerg & Swinbank, 2015; Gössling & Hall, 2013). Secondly, one of the responses to the challenges of the EU's common agricultural policy has been to introduce a wider focus on rural development, with place-based rural development policies that are supposed to bolster the economic and social robustness of local communities (Kull, 2014).

In Denmark this has resulted in bottom-up activities in the form of, in particular, producer network initiatives such as the *Smagen af Danmark* networks, supported by European rural development funding, which in some cases also attempt to associate tourist destinations with local food, especially local produce rather than local culinary traditions (Jørgensen et al., 2015; Thuesen, Ditlevsen, & Kromann, 2014). Unsurprisingly, these locally driven initiatives have resulted in a rather uneven pattern of activity across the country, and it is instructive to contrast the efforts of two peripheral parts of Denmark both wanting to position themselves on the basis of local food. The Baltic island of Bornholm has pursued a comprehensive and persistent strategy towards branding the island through the development of a wide range of food and drink products. These are available not only to locals and the large number of visiting tourists in the summer season, but also in supermarkets in Copenhagen and beyond (Manniche & Larsen, 2013). Conversely, in North Jutland, another major coastal holiday destination with a rural hinterland, efforts have been less coherent: forming networks between existing producers and publicizing their offerings have been prioritized in a series of on–off projects. Less effort has been devoted to increasing the production of local food and making it available to residents and visitors (Jørgensen et al., 2015). As the array of instruments and level of funding available to policy-makers in peripheral regions are by and large comparable, this difference reflects different degrees of priority accorded by the two regions to local food compared to other economic development strategies.

Similarly, in Sweden the national initiative *Matlandet Sverige* has helped move local food higher up on the agenda in regional and rural development. Here the extent to which this is prioritized also varies, although, interestingly, it is not restricted to the fertile lowlands of southern Sweden. To the south, Skåne has retained its prominent position as a provider of a vast array of food with traditional strongholds such as apple-related produce supported through subregional networks in order to promote local produce and products (Backe, 2013; Olsson, 2015). However, in northern Jämtland with its less hospitable climate, local food has also become a major element in the regional economic development strategy. This includes an event-based branding strategy, the New Nordic two Michelin star *Fäviken* restaurant, advanced training for new producers at the *Eldrimner* National Resource Centre for Food Crafts and measures designed to encourage new producers to enter the market (Rytkönen, Bonow, Johansson, & Persson, 2013). These cases demonstrate the importance of local food in Swedish regions, even if the conditions are less advantageous in terms of competing priorities (Skåne) or climate (Jämtland).

In Norway, specialty food developed as a differentiation strategy for farmers and rural areas in the 1990s, and thus local food became an integrated part of the dominant rural development policy discourse in Norway (Landbruks- og matdepartementet 2011). Moreover, the Norwegian policy for the development of local food also includes tools and incentives for regional and local initiatives. Authorities at the county level have initiated projects to stimulate the establishment and expansion of processors of local food and other food specialties. As a part of the VSP programme, five regional competence centres were established. Another example of a valuable effect of a bottom-up action supported by public resources is the mountainous region of Røros which has achieved great success with local food (Kvam, Holmen, & Pedersen, 2015; Lange-Vik & Idsø, 2013): over the last 20 years, a number of local food firms of various kinds have established and expanded their production and value added. Thirty of them are members of a cooperative, *Rørosmat*, that offers distribution of local food products and owns their regional brand *Røros – mat fra Rørostraktene/Røros* (food from the region of Røros). A good mix of local cooperation and networking, local enthusiasts and governmental support is important in explaining this development.

5. Conclusions

In this paper, we have presented a comparative analysis of the development and governance of specialty food in Denmark, Norway and Sweden. We have developed a definition of specialty food that incorporates two main dimensions: (a) localization, which includes distance between producers and final consumers, as well as local recipes or place-specific production methods; and (b) specialization, which refers to production and processing methods that depart from industrialized mass production, for example, organic or artisan production.

We have used a number of indicators to compare these dimensions in the three countries, and reviewed policy and academic literature on the governance of the food sector. This analysis shows that specialty food has increased in importance in all three countries over the last twenty years, but there are important differences in the kind of specialty food that has developed most and the nature of government intervention and governance structures.

Overall, Sweden appears to have the largest production of specialty food and drink, and is particularly strong in organic production and consumption, farm processing and farm shops. Norway has a large number of products with protected origin and also leads in the number of farmers' markets. In terms of the limited range of indicators evaluated here, Denmark lags behind the other countries, but has witnessed the fastest growth in microbreweries over the last five years.

In terms of stimulating producers to engage in specialized food production, public policies with regard to organics appear to have been broadly similar, with early certification and labelling schemes in place in all three countries, which were then backed up by government schemes that assisted the conversion from traditional to organic production methods. Conversely, with regard to microbreweries, there seems to have been little direct government support for small-scale or artisan brewing. However, specialized production methods are covered indirectly by policy support for small enterprises and, in Norway, 'local food' policies.

Policy differences between the countries are noticeable with regard to 'local' food. Danish efforts focus on regional/local networks between producers, while Sweden has seen more extensive national efforts with considerable variation between regions. Norway seems to have made the most extensive and sustained efforts with regard to making it more attractive for producers to join the move towards more local food, which has a broad definition including food produced using traditional methods or from a particular origin (rather than focusing only on distance from producers to market). There is also a clear difference between Norway and the other two countries in the importance attached to the certification of specialty food products from particular places, with Norway having instituted its own extensive set of protection labels. While there are some regional certification schemes in operation in the other two countries, both use the European certification scheme at a national scale and have very few products registered.

In terms of attempts to influence consumer demand, Denmark has made most use of the New Nordic concept, both in terms of promoting its supposed health benefits and in tourism marketing. Sweden has also attempted to raise the profile of the country's food offer through marketing and the *Matlandet* campaign, which focused on both production and consumption (e.g. by encouraging public institutions to procure food locally), while in Norway there appears to be little consumer-focused policy in operation.

Overall, then, there appear to be some clear differences between these three countries which highlight the importance of distinguishing between different kinds of specialty food. While the New Nordic concept, combining local and sustainable/organic qualities, is widely recognized and draws on many of the trends identified in our analysis, the reality of specialty food production and consumption in the Scandinavian countries is varied. This suggests that from both an analytical and a policy perspective, moving beyond broad categories such as 'alternative' or 'specialty' food will help to further our understanding of new trends – and, indeed, attempts to influence future developments – in food production and consumption. In pursuing a more nuanced conceptualization of specialty food, it is also important to remember that definitions change over time. Before the advent of industrialized agriculture, for example, food produced without the use of pesticides or industrial fertilizers was certainly not alternative. Equally, what may be considered speciality according to one set of criteria may not be in another. Thus, a microbrewery may be small scale and produce a 'local' style beer, but may use a similar technology to a larger producer. Another example is the varying definitions of 'local' used in different countries which also highlights the potential difficulties in expanding the specialty food sector. The Swedish definition of local food based on the geographical distance between producers and retailers implies that local food cannot be exported, but only scaled up by developing local food in every community. By contrast, Norwegian 'local food' refers to distinct qualities embodied in a food product which could be exported.

Despite these changing dynamics, it is also important to stress that commonalities exist that point towards the possible existence of a 'Scandinavian model' of specialty food governance with extensive interaction between central government, local government and private firms to stimulate the growth of specialty food, characteristics that set these countries apart from the ideal types derived from the market-based Anglo-Saxon and statist European experiences. However, how different Scandinavia is from other 'mixed' forms of governance as found in, for example, North Western Europe (Everett & Slocum, 2013; Sims, 2009) or Canada (Telfer & Hashimoto, 2013) cannot be ascertained on the basis of the current evidence. In order to achieve this, much better international comparative data on the production, consumption and governance of local food are required.

Disclosure statement

No potential conflict of interest was reported by the authors.

References

Almås, R. (2004). *Norwegian agricultural history*. Trondheim: Tapir Academic.
Backe, J. Ø. (2013). Culinary networks and rural tourism development – Constructing the local through everyday practices. In C. M. Hall & S. Gossling (Eds.), *Sustainable culinary systems: Local foods, innovation, tourism and hospitality* (pp. 47–63). Abingdon: Routledge.
Becker, T., & Staus, A. (2009). European food quality policy: The importance of geographical indications, organic certification and food quality assurance schemes in European countries. *The Estey Centre Journal of International Law and Trade Policy*, *10*(1), 111–130. Retrieved from http://law.usask.ca/research/estey-journal/
Bjørkhaug, H., & Kvam, G. T. (2011). Local small-scale food enterprises: Ambitions and initiatives for achieving business growth among male and female owners and managers. *Ager*, (11), 29–55. Retrieved from http://www.redalyc.org/articulo.oa?id=29620045002
Bonow, M., & Rytkönen, P. (2012). Gastronomy and tourism as a regional development tool-the case of Jämtland. *Advances in Food, Hospitality and Tourism*, *2*(1), 2–10.
Bondens Marked. (2016). Retrieved from http://bondensmarked.no/.

Bryggeri- og drikkevareforeningen. (2016). *Numbers given in e-mail from Petter Nome*. Retrieved January 15, 2016, from http://urn.kb.se/resolve?urn=urn:nbn:se:sh:diva-21112.

Byrkjeflot, H., Pedersen, J. S., & Svejenova, S. (2013). From label to practice: The process of creating new Nordic cuisine. *Journal of Culinary Science & Technology, 11*(1), 36–55. doi:10.1080/15428052.2013.754296

Che, D., Week, A., & Veeck, G. (2005). Sustaining production and strengthening the agritourism product: Linkages among Michigan agritourism destinations. *Agriculture and Human Values, 22*(2), 225–234. doi:10.1007/s10460-004-8282-0

Coenen, L., & Moodysson, J. (2009). Putting constructed regional advantage into Swedish practice. *European Planning Studies, 17*(4), 587–604. doi:10.1080/09654310802682180

Cooke, P. (2016). Nordic innovation models: Why is Norway different? *Norsk Geografisk Tidsskrift – Norwegian Journal of Geography*, 1–12. doi:10.1080/00291951.2016.1167120

Cox, R. (2004). The path-dependency of an idea: Why Scandinavian welfare states remain distinct. *Social Policy & Administration, 38*(2), 204–219. doi:10.1111/j.1467-9515.2004.00386.x

Dagens Opinion. (2015). *Regeringen lovar ny livsmedelsstrategi om ett år – Eskil Erlandsson (c) rasar*. Retrieved from http://dagensopinion.se/regeringen-lovar-ny-livsmedelsstrategi-om-%C3%A5r-%E2%80%93-eskil-erlandsson-c-rasar

Danske Regioner. (2011). *Fødevareudvikling i fem regioner*. København: Author.

Daugbjerg, C., & Svendsen, G. T. (2010). Government intervention in green industries: Lessons from the wind turbine and the organic food industries in Denmark. *Environment, Development and Sustainability, 13*(2), 293–307. doi:10.1007/s10668-010-9262-8

Daugbjerg, C., & Swinbank, A. (2015). Three decades of policy layering and politically sustainable reform in the European Union's agricultural policy. *Governance*. doi:10.1111/gove.12171

DG Agriculture. (2016). *Agricultural products and foodstuffs – PDO and PGI – Reg. (EC) No 510/2006 EU 27*. Retrieved January 24, 2016, from http://ec.europa.eu/agriculture/quality/schemes/index_en.htm

Eriksen, S. N., & Sundbo, J. (2015). Drivers and barriers to the development of local food networks in rural Denmark. *European Urban and Regional Studies*. doi:10.1177/0969776414567971

Esping-Andersen, G. (1990). *Three worlds of welfare capitalism*. London: John Wiley.

Everett, S., & Aitchison, C. (2008). The role of food tourism in sustaining regional identity: A case study of Cornwall, South West England. *Journal of Sustainable Tourism, 16*(2), 150–167. doi:10.2167/jost696.0

Everett, S., & Slocum, S. L. (2013). Collaboration in food tourism: Developing cross-industry partners. In C. M. Hall & S. Gossling (Eds.), *Sustainable culinary systems: Local foods, innovation, tourism and hospitality* (pp. 205–222). Abingdon: Routledge.

Feldmann, C., & Hamm, U. (2015). Consumers' perceptions and preferences for local food: A review. *Food Quality and Preference, 40*, 152–164. doi:10.1016/j.foodqual.2014.09.014

Goodman, D. (2003). The quality 'turn' and alternative food practices: Reflections and agenda. *Journal of Rural Studies, 19*, 1–7. doi:10.1016/S0743-0167(02)00043-8

Gössling, S., & Hall, C. M. (2013). Sustainable culinary systems: An introduction. In C. M. Hall & S. Gössling (Eds.), *Sustainable culinary systems: Local foods, innovation, tourism and hospitality* (pp. 3–42). Abingdon: Routledge.

HANEN. (2016). *Genuint, ekte og smakfullt. Opplev Norge*. Retrieved from http://www.hanen.no/

Hantrais, L. (2009). *International comparative research: Theory, methods and practice*. London: Palgrave.

He, C., & Mikkelsen, B. E. (2014). The association between organic school food policy and school food environment: Results from an observational study in Danish schools. *Perspectives in Public Health, 134*(2), 110–116. doi:10.1177/1757913913517976

Hegnes, A. W. (2013). *Kulturelt tilpasningsarbeid: Innføring, forvaltning og bruk av merkeordningen Beskyttede betegnelser i Norge* (PhD). Department of Sociology and Human Geography, Faculty of Social Sciences, University of Oslo, Oslo.

Hegnes, A. W. (2015). Mentalt grensevern for norske landbruksprodukter: Kulturelt tilpasningsarbeid i tre akter. In H. Bjørkhaug, R. Almås, & J. Vik (Eds.), *Norsk matmakt i endring* (pp. 221–241). Bergen: Fagbokforlaget.

Henriksen, P. F., & Halkier, H. (2015). Feeding countryside tourists: Exploring collaborative actor strategies in rural Denmark. In K. Dashper (Ed.), *Rural tourism – An international perspective* (pp. 250–266). Newcastle upon Tyne: Cambridge Scholars.

Holmqvist, A. (2013). *Eskils miljardflopp – 10 000 jobb borta*. Retrieved February 4, 2016, from http://www.aftonbladet.se/nyheter/article17824554.ab

Ingebritsen, C. (2002). The Scandinavian way and its legacy in Europe. *Scandinavian Studies*, 74(3), 255–264. Retrieved from http://www.jstor.org/stable/40920388

Ingemann, J. H. (2006). The evolution of organic agriculture in Denmark. *Working Paper from Department of Economics, Politics and Public Administration Aalborg University*, 2006(4), 1–53. Retrieved from http://vbn.aau.dk/files/32239837/2010-2-Jan-H-Ingemann-2%20rådne%20banan.pdf

Innovasjon Norge. (2016). Retrieved February 2, 2016, from http://www.innovasjonnorge.no/no/landbruk/Tjenester/nye-lokalmat-sider/lokalmat--og-drikke2/#.VrEr3bLhAdU

James, L., & Halkier, H. (2014). Regional development platforms and related variety: Exploring the changing practices of food tourism in North Jutland, Denmark. *European Urban and Regional Studies*. Advance online publication. doi:10.1177/0969776414557293

Jordbruksverket. (2010). *Matlandet ur ett regionalt perspektiv* (No. 2010:13) (pp. 1–50). Jönköping.

Jordbruksverket. (2013). *Sverige – det nya Matlandet 2014* (pp. 1–292). Jönköping: Jordbruksverket.

Jordbruksverket. (2016). *Smake Sverige: Nätverk*. Retrieved from http://smakasverige.jordbruksverket.se/natverk.38.html#query/*%3A*

Jørgensen, T., Halkier, H., & James, H. (2015). *Produktion af madoplevelser for kystturister: Fire danske case-studier*. Aalborg: Aalborg Universitet & Center for Kystturisme.

Kjeldsen, C., Deleuran, L. C., & Noe, E. (2013). The quality turn in the Danish food scape: New food chains emerging – new territorial impacts? *Acta Agriculturae Scandinavica Section B – Soil and Plant Science*, 63(Suppl. 1), 19–28. doi:10.1080/09064710.2013.789549

Kjus, J., Utgård, J., Pettersen, I., Svennerud, M., & Eriksen, L. Ø. (2009). *Matprogram med næringsverdi: Evaluering av bedriftsrettede prosjekter i Verdiskapingsprogrammet for matproduksjon og Nettverksprogrammet* (Rapport 2009-1). Oslo: NILF.

KRAV. (2016). *KRAV in English*. Retrieved January 17, 2016, from http://www.krav.se/english

Kull, M. (2014). *European integration and rural development*. Farnham: Ashgate.

Kvam, G. T., Holmen, E., & Pedersen, A. C. (2015). Managing in a regional network: The case of regional development in the Røros area. IMP workshop: Policy making in an interactive business world; 2015-05-26–2015-05-28.

Kvam, G.-T., & Magnus, T. (2011). Kvalitetsstrategier ved vekst – erfaringer fra fem nisjematbedrifter. In M. S. Haugen & E. P. Stræte (Eds.), *Rurale brytninger* (pp. 381–404). Trondheim: Tapir Akademiske Forlag.

Kvam, G.-T., Magnus, T., & Stræte, E. P. (2014). Product strategies for growth in niche food firms. *British Food Journal*, 116(4), 723–732. doi:10.1108/BFJ-06-2011-0168

Landbruksdepartementet. (2001). *Verdiskapingsprogrammet for matproduksjon. et program for innovasjon og mangfold på matområdet*. Report from a working group.

Landbruks- og matdepartementet. (2011). *Meld. St. 9 (2011–2012) Landbruks- og matpolitikken – Velkommen til bords*. Oslo.

Landbruks- og matdepartementet. (2015). *Kraftig økning i salg av lokalmat*. Retrieved from https://www.regjeringen.no/no/aktuelt/kraftig-okning-i-salg-av-lokalmat/id2459431/

Lange-Vik, M., & Idsø, J. (2013). Rørosmat: The development and success of a local food brand in Norway. In C. M. Hall & S. Gössling (Eds.), *Sustainable culinary systems: Local foods, innovation, tourism and hospitality* (pp. 85–98). Abingdon: Routledge.

Lantbrukarnas Riksforbund. (2015). *En livsmedelsstrategi för Sverige*. Stockholm.

Manniche, J. (2008). *Den rumlige fordeling og udvikling af fødevaresektoren i Danmark – typer af landdistrikter og kommuner* (pp. 1–45). Nexø: CRT.

Manniche, J. (2010). Production-consumption models and knowledge dynamics in the food and drinks sector. In P. Cooke, C. de Laurentis, C. Collinge, & S. MacNeill (Eds.), *Platforms of innovation: Dynamics of new industrial knowledge flows* (pp. 53–78). London: Edward Elgar.

Manniche, J., & Larsen, K. T. (2013). Experience staging and symbolic knowledge: The case of Bornholm culinary products. *European Urban and Regional Studies, 20*(4), 401–416. doi:10.1177/0969776412453146

Marsden, T., & Smith, E. (2005). Ecological entrepreneurship: Sustainable development in local communities through quality food production and local branding. *Geoforum, 36*(4), 440–451. doi:10.1016/j.geoforum.2004.07.008

Matmerk. (2016a). *Lokalmat – Velkommen.* Retrieved from https://www.lokalmat.no/no

Matmerk. (2016b). Retrieved January 27, 2016, from http://matmerk.no/no/matmerk/aktuelt/kraftig-oekning-i-salg-av-lokalmat

Matmerk. (2016c). Retrieved February 20, 2016, from http://www.matmerk.no/no/spesialitet/om-spesialitet

Mat- och Jordbruksnätverket Naturskyddsföreningen. (2012). *Sverige – det nya Matlandet?* Retrieved from https://matochjordbruksnatverket.wordpress.com/2012/06/25/sverige-det-nya-matlandet/

Micheelsen, A., Holm, L., & Jensen, K. O. (2013). Consumer acceptance of the New Nordic Diet. An exploratory study. *Appetite, 70*(C), 14–21. doi:10.1016/j.appet.2013.06.081

Morris, C., & Young, C. (2000). 'Seed to shelf', 'teat to table', 'barley to beer' and 'womb to tomb': Discourses of food quality and quality assurance schemes in the UK. *Journal of Rural Studies, 16*, 103–115. doi:10.1016/S0743-0167(99)00044-3

Murdoch, J., Marsden, T., & Banks, J. (2000). Quality, nature, and embeddedness: Some theoretical considerations in the context of the food sector. *Economic Geography, 76*(2), 107–125. doi:10.2307/144549

Nordic Council. (2015). Retrieved September 16, 2015, from http://www.norden.org/en/news-and-events/news/new-nordic-food-at-the-un-cooking-for-a-sustainable-future

Olsson, V. (2015). Local and regional food – perspectives from the south Baltic region of Sweden. In A. Petrenko & B. Müller-Hansen (Eds.), *Interdisciplinary perspectives on local and regional food in the South Baltic region* (pp. 45–57). Kristianstad: Kristianstad University Press.

O'Reilly, S., & Haines, M. (2004). Marketing quality food products – A comparison of two SME marketing networks. *Acta Agriculturae Scandinavica, Section C — Food Economics, 1*(3), 137–150. doi:10.1080/16507540410035027

Parrott, N., Wilson, N., & Murdoch, J. (2002). Spatialising quality: Regional protection and the alternative geography of food. *European Urban and Regional Studies, 9*(3), 241–261. doi:10.1177/096977640200900304

Regeringen. (2012). *Økologisk Handlingsplan 2020* (pp. 1–19). Ministeriet for Fødevarer, Landbrug og Fiskeri.

Renting, H., Marsden, T. K., & Banks, J. (2003). Understanding alternative food networks: Exploring the role of short food supply chains in rural development. *Environment & Planning A, 35*(3), 393–411.

Roininen, K., Arvola, A., & Lähteenmäki, L. (2006). Exploring consumers' perceptions of local food with two different qualitative techniques: Laddering and word association. *Food Quality and Preference, 17*(1–2), 20–30. doi:10.1016/j.foodqual.2005.04.012

Rytkönen, P., Bonow, M., Johansson, M., & Persson, Y. (2013). Goat cheese production in Sweden – A pioneering experience in the re-emergence of local food. *Acta Agriculturae Scandinavica Section B – Soil and Plant Science, 63*(Suppl. 1), 38–46. doi:10.1080/09064710.2013.798682

Sims, R. (2009). Food, place and authenticity: Local food and the sustainable tourism experience. *Journal of Sustainable Tourism, 17*(3), 321–336. doi:10.1080/09669580802359293

Storstad, O. (2008). Det nasjonale i det globale. Nasjonale, lokale og rurale symboler i markedsføringen av mat. In R. Almås, M. S. Haugen, J. F. Rye, & M. Villa Trondheim (Eds.), *Den nye bygda* (pp. 65–83). Trondheim: Tapir Akademisk Forlag.

Stræte, E. P. (2008). Modes of qualities in development of speciality food. *British Food Journal, 110* (1), 62–75. doi:10.1108/00070700810844795

Stræte, E. P. (2016). Quality as a competitive advantage for the rural food industry. In A. Lindgreen, M. K. Hingley, R. J. Angell, J. Memery, & J. Vanhamme (Eds.), *A stakeholder approach to managing food: Local, national, and global issues* (pp. 241–255). Farnham: Gower.

Telfer, D. J., & Hashimoto, A. (2013). Raising awareness of local food through tourism as sustainable development: Lessons from Japan and Canada. In C. M. Hall & S. Gossling (Eds.), *Sustainable culinary systems: Local foods, innovation, tourism and hospitality* (pp. 168–186). Abingdon: Routledge.

Testa, S. (2011). Internationalization patterns among speciality food companies: Some Italian case study evidence. *British Food Journal, 113*(11), 1406–1426. doi:10.1108/00070701111180012

The Brewers of Europe. (2014). *Beer statistics 2014 edition.* Brussels: The Brewers of Europe.

The Brewers of Europe. (2015). *Beer statistics 2015 edition.* Brussels: The Brewers of Europe.

Therkelsen, A., & Blichfeldt, B. S. (2012). Understanding tourists' complex food relations. In M. Mair & D. Wagner (Eds.), *Culinary tourism: Products, regions, tourists* (pp. 119–128). Vienna: Springer.

Therkelsen, A., & Halkier, H. (2015). *Lokale fødevare- og madoplevelser på danske kystdestinationer.* Aalborg: Department of Culture and Global Studies, Aalborg University.

Thorsøe, M. H., Kjeldsen, C., & Noe, E. (in press). It's never too late to join the revolution! Enabling new modes of production in the contemporary Danish food system. *European Planning Studies* Special Issue XXXX.

Thuesen, A. A., Ditlevsen, S. E., & Kromann, D. S. (2014). *Evaluering af LAG-udviklingsstrategierne under Landdistriktsprogrammet og Fiskeriudviklingsprogrammet 2007-2013. Anbefalinger for perioden 2014-2020.* Esbjerg: Center for Landdistriktsforskning, SDU.

Tranholm, H., & Halkier, H. (2015). *Danish events database.* Aalborg: Tourism Research Unit, Aalborg University.

Tregear, A. (2011). Progressing knowledge in alternative and local food networks: Critical reflections and a research agenda. *Journal of Rural Studies, 27*(4), 419–430. doi:10.1016/j.jrurstud.2011.06.003

Tregear, A., Arfini, F., Belletti, G., & Marescotti, A. (2007). Regional foods and rural development: The role of product qualification. *Journal of Rural Studies, 23*(1), 12–22. doi:10.1016/j.jrurstud.2006.09.010

Vik, J., & McElwee, G. (2011). Diversification and the entrepreneurial motivations of farmers in Norway. *Journal of Small Business Management, 49*(3), 390–410.

Vittersø, G., & Jervell, A. M. (2011). Direct markets as multiple consumption spaces: The case of two Norwegian collective marketing initiatives. *International Journal of Sociology of Agriculture and Food, 18*(1), 54–69. Retrieved from http://www.ijsaf.org/archive/18/1/vitterso_jervell.pdf

Wiborg, S. (2013). Neo-liberalism and universal state education: The cases of Denmark, Norway and Sweden 1980-2011. *Comparative Education, 49*(4), 407–423. doi:10.1080/03050068.2012.700436

Sustainability transformations in the balance: exploring Swedish initiatives challenging the corporate food regime

Jacob von Oelreich and Rebecka Milestad

ABSTRACT
This paper explores to what extent organic initiatives that go beyond mainstream organic (so-called Organic 3.0) can challenge the corporate food regime and how they can push the food system towards sustainability transformations. We depart from the assumption that individual initiatives may differ in their potential to influence the corporate food regime and that this potential can be assessed by examining traits linked to reformist, progressive or radical food regime/food movement trends that they may possess. Rather than establishing a dichotomy between niche and food regime or categorizing Organic 3.0 initiatives within one of these trends, we explore the nuances in niche–regime relationships within the food system from a multi-level perspective, using the cases of two Organic 3.0 initiatives in Sweden. The results show that relations between these initiatives and the food regime share key characteristics, but also differ in important respects. While a reformist strategy facilitates niche growth, progressive and radical approaches are more likely to challenge the regime. The choice of approach in both cases involves trade-offs between growth and organic values. We conclude that one of the primary roles of Organic 3.0 initiatives may be to illustrate the viability of alternative models.

Introduction

In the present context of compounded environmental, climate, socio-economic and geo-political crisis, there is a need for radical, systemic sustainability transformations (Olsson, Galaz, & Boonstra, 2014; Raskin et al., 2002), not least in the global food system (Hinrichs, 2014; Marsden, 2013). This system faces a 'quadruple squeeze' from anthropogenic climate change, increased population and development pressures, ecosystem crises and the risk of transgressing the safe operating space of the Earth system (Rockström & Karlberg, 2010). The requirement for a sustainable food system that meets the dietary needs of the world's population will not be met by business-as-usual production in industrialized agriculture (IAASTD, 2008).

Organic agriculture challenges the conventional food system and suggests alternative, environmentally and socially benign ways of producing food (Allen & Kovach, 2000;

Dantsi, Loumou, & Giourga, 2009; Goldberger, 2011). The first wave of organic farming, 'Organic 1.0', driven by organic pioneers and emerging about a century ago, led on to the emergence of a common organic movement from the 1970s and onwards. This movement, 'Organic 2.0', currently forms the organic mainstream and is characterized by reliance on organic standards and certification. It constitutes a niche in the overall food system, but this niche is growing and diversifying. Mainstream organics is being challenged by 'Organic 3.0', which aims for a new level of sustainability, complementing previous approaches with a stronger focus on systemic impact in terms of health, ecology, fairness and care (Arbenz, Gould, & Stopes, 2015; Gould, 2015). A multitude of emerging Organic 3.0 initiatives are part of wider food movements to varying degrees, and embedded within the social economy (Seyfang & Smith, 2007). Thus, Organic 3.0 can be seen as a 'niche within a niche', proposing reinterpretation of sustainability and of what organic agriculture should be about.

A sustainability transformation requires change on multiple levels (Olsson et al., 2014). In other words, macro, meso and micro levels need to be connected. Macro-level pressures such as climate change and resource depletion can be leveraged by micro-level niches in challenging dominant meso-level regimes (Darnhofer, 2015; Marsden, 2013). However, niches can also be challenged from within, as in the case of Organic 3.0 challenging mainstream organics.

The current global food system is dominated by a corporate food regime characterized by prevailing neoliberal and reformist trends (Holt Giménez & Shattuck, 2011). Mainstream organics occupies a niche within this system, whereas Organic 3.0 initiatives are linked to progressive and radical trends within the global food system that aim for 'metamorphosis' (Gould, 2015, p. 140) of the organic approach and of the overall system.

Thus, alternative food practices are emerging within the global food system (Davidson, Jones, & Parkins, 2016), creating a niche encompassing organic farming and organic food initiatives challenging mainstream conventional agriculture (Allen & Kovach, 2000; Dantsi et al., 2009; Goldberger, 2011). However, such practices and initiatives struggle to influence the overall regime (Holt Giménez & Shattuck, 2011). The questions we explore in this paper are what potential influence Organic 3.0 initiatives can have on the corporate food regime, how they can push both the organic niche and the overall food system towards sustainability transformations, and whether various initiatives differ in their potential in this regard. We operationalize these questions by analysing two Organic 3.0 food initiatives in Sweden along two dimensions: their position within major food regime/food movement trends (Holt Giménez & Shattuck, 2011) and their transformational potential in terms of influencing the organic niche and corporate food regime (Seyfang & Haxeltine, 2012). In turn, we operationalize the first dimension through analysing the basic orientation of the initiatives, their beneficiaries, their geographical scope, the solutions they provide and the types of food they advocate (Holt Giménez & Shattuck, 2011), and the second dimension through analysing the potential of the initiatives to influence the organic niche and corporate food regime through growth, replication, learning and questioning the regime (Seyfang & Haxeltine, 2012). Our assumption is that individual Organic 3.0 initiatives influence the organic niche and corporate food regime differently by possessing traits attributable to more or less reformist, progressive and radical trends (Holt Giménez & Shattuck, 2011). We explore differences between cases by studying individual initiatives at the micro level, where contrasts can be discerned, making the link between the meso (regime) and micro (niche initiative) levels, applying a multi-level perspective (MLP) (Darnhofer, 2015; Geels, 2011; Marsden, 2013).

Transformation of the corporate food regime

Acknowledging the urgent need for transformations to sustainability (Olsson et al., 2014; Raskin et al., 2002) raises the question of how change can come about. Within transitions thinking, the MLP explains change in terms of interactions between landscape, regimes and niches (Darnhofer, 2015). Understanding the possibilities for change requires analysis of all three levels. While climate change, environmental degradation and food insecurity are central issues in the current food landscape, the role of niches in spurring transformation through social innovation and the introduction of novelties is a key concern in the MLP (Marsden, 2013; van der Ploeg et al., 2004). Transitional processes require 'the gradual but persistent creation' of niches (van der Ploeg et al., 2004, p. 10). Situated between landscape and niches, the 'regime level is of primary interest, because transitions are defined as shifts from one regime to another' (Geels, 2011, p. 26). The current food regime experiences pressure from the macro (landscape) and micro (niche) levels, in terms of crisis and innovative disruption, respectively (Marsden, 2013). To identify ways in which niches could influence or shift the dominant food regime, closer analysis of the prevailing regime and its counter-movements is required.

The corporate food regime can be characterized as a 'rule-governed structure of production and consumption of food on a world scale' (Friedmann, 1993, pp. 30–31), underpinned by neoliberal policies and corporate domination (McMichael, 2014). Thus, in addition to the 'tangible and measurable' components of a system, a regime also encompasses 'intangible and underlying deep structures', such as norms and beliefs (Geels, 2011, p. 31). Growing opposition to the corporate food regime can be seen as intrinsic to the regime, bringing with it the emergence of progressive and radical alternatives (Holt Giménez & Shattuck, 2011), thus providing potential for transformation (Bernstein, 2015). According to Holt Giménez and Shattuck (2011), the corporate food regime is based on 'neoliberal' and 'reformist' trends, while emerging food movements represent 'progressive' and 'radical' trends (Figure 1).

The 'neoliberal' trend is global in scope and dominates the corporate food regime. It is characterized by corporate concentration and deregulation of global markets, with its proponents advocating increased industrial production and high-input agriculture. The food produced through the neoliberal model is industrial food for mass global consumption (Holt Giménez & Shattuck, 2011). The 'reformist' trend supports partial regulation of markets, maintenance of agricultural subsidies and certification of niche markets, such as organic, fair trade and local food. Farmers of the Global North benefit from the reformist trend through subsidies. The geographical scope of the reformist approach is global, but also

CURRENT GLOBAL FOOD SYSTEM			
CORPORATE FOOD REGIME		FOOD MOVEMENTS	
Neoliberal trend	Reformist trend	Progressive trend	Radical trend

Figure 1. Simplified representation of the food regime/food movement framework proposed by Holt Giménez and Shattuck (2011).

regional (e.g. European Union (EU)), national and local. It promotes industrial, quality food and food production under various forms of certification (2011). While it strives to modify the food regime through reform, it represents 'a fine-tuning of the neoliberal project rather than a substantive change of direction' towards sustainability transformations (2011, p. 124).

The 'progressive' trend advocates regulated markets and solidarity to enable empowerment of farmers, farming communities and agricultural workers. It has a focus on the local level and is promoted by food justice, family farming and agro-ecological movements. Key considerations include the right to food, sustainably produced local food and improved social conditions for workers and communities (Holt Giménez & Shattuck, 2011). In terms of food, it emphasizes agro-ecologically produced, good, clean and fair food, pleasure, quality and authenticity. The 'radical' trend aims at transforming the entire global food system. It 'seeks deep, structural changes to food and agriculture' and demands 'a radical transformation of society' (2011, p. 128). It is represented primarily by food sovereignty movements and its main beneficiaries are peasants, small-scale farmers and farming communities. It embraces the idea of local and regional food systems. Radical food movements support the dismantling of corporate monopolies and power, the introduction of democratic control over the food system, wealth redistribution, land reform, agroecology and climate action. In terms of food, the radical approach emphasizes agro-ecologically and sustainably produced food.

Holt Giménez and Shattuck (2011) place the progressive and radical trends of global food movements beyond the corporate food regime, 'not because they are separate, autonomous or somehow autarchic, but in order to assess their potential to influence the regime' (2011, p. 116). They argue that social movements part of progressive and radical trends within the food system need to exert joint 'social pressure' and advance common political goals to bring about change (2011, p. 136). Similarly, Geels (2010) argues that transitions to sustainability in terms of resolving global environmental problems require the involvement of social movements and public opinion.

The categorization by Holt Giménez and Shattuck (2011) of organizations striving for community benefit as progressive or radical movements closely relates to Seyfang and Smith's (2007) notion of 'the social economy' as an alternative niche where surplus is reinvested rather than appropriated by capital. From the MLP, the social economy can be understood as a niche where 'the rules are different' (2007, p. 591). Niches offer protected spaces (Seyfang & Haxeltine, 2012) facilitating approaches based on alternative 'social, ethical and cultural rules' (Seyfang & Smith, 2007). However, it is questionable whether rules can be truly different under a hegemonic regime, illustrating the paradoxical relationship between niche and regime. The niche can be seen as both separate from, and part of, the regime, since by building alternatives, niches are intrinsically linked to the regime (Bernstein, 2015). Pressure from niches on the regime can take several forms (Seyfang & Haxeltine, 2012). Growth can occur through scaling up of individual initiatives within a niche, existing initiatives within the niche can be replicated and emergence of a multitude of initiatives can generate cumulative change. Furthermore, ideas and practices emerging within the niche can be translated into the regime. Finally, learning within a niche can be transferred to the regime or used to question its very existence (2012). Niche influence on the regime depends on the potential of alternative niche initiatives to inspire other initiatives to follow their example and on their capacity to illustrate their viability as alternative models (Hendrickson & Heffernan, 2002).

Resistance to the hegemonic food regime is exerted by a multitude of food movements, including the organic movement. However, organics exists mainly within the reformist strand of the corporate food regime, where its transformational capacity is debatable (Holt Giménez & Shattuck, 2011). The heated discussion about conventionalization of organic agriculture is a case in point (see Goldberger, 2011; Schewe, 2014, for reviews). The 'conventionalization hypothesis' states that organic farming is moving away from ecological integrity, progressive values and transformational potential. Others report a bifurcation of the organic movement, with the part that remains non-conventionalized still celebrating artisanal production, local markets and deeply held values (Goldberger, 2011). However, the validity of these claims and the usefulness of binary thinking have been questioned (Rosin & Campbell, 2009; Schewe, 2014). Instead, Rosin and Campbell (2009) call for more complex theoretical frameworks to analyse the worlds of organic agriculture, as attempted in this study.

A wide range of organic initiatives and enterprises claim to go beyond current organic standards towards Organic 3.0, which in an EU context means exceeding EU organic regulations. Consequently, Organic 3.0 can be seen as an emerging 'alternative within the alternative', or 'niche within a niche'. Holt Giménez and Shattuck (2011) describe food movements as alternatives to the corporate food regime. However, Organic 3.0 is not simply a food movement, but rather a multitude of alternative food initiatives that are part of wider food movements to varying degrees (Davidson et al., 2016). Shared features of Organic 3.0 initiatives are their positioning within the social economy, where surplus is reinvested within the initiative (Seyfang & Smith, 2007), and their commitment to deeper sustainability (Gould, 2015).

To enable transformations towards a sustainable food system, the Organic 3.0 niche needs to influence both the wider organic niche and the overall regime. Such influence may take the form of 'linking' or 'anchoring', whereby novel practices are translated into the wider niche or regime (Elzen, van Mierlo, & Leeuwis, 2012). This transformational development has been described as turning organic farming into 'the mainstream choice for agriculture [...] but also its leading edge' (Gould, 2015, p. 137), that is, transforming the regime towards organic, while at the same time moving Organic 2.0 towards Organic 3.0. In analysis of this multifaceted, multi-level process, we move from the niche to the level of individual Organic 3.0 initiatives, which can be seen as niche 'actors'. Holt Giménez and Shattuck (2011) argue that individual initiatives can exert meaningful (joint) pressure on the regime only through contributing to the joint social movement of progressive and radical initiatives. Thus, the transformational potential of an individual initiative depends on its approach (cf. Bui, Cardona, Lamine, & Cerf, 2016). The potential of Organic 3.0 niche initiatives for growth, replication, learning and questioning the regime (Seyfang & Haxeltine, 2012) may therefore depend on their reformist, progressive and radical traits. Identifying reformist, progressive and radical features of different initiatives can reveal their potential to influence the food regime and help achieve transformations towards sustainability.

Organic farming in Sweden

Since 1970, the number of farms in Sweden has halved, farm size has grown significantly and production volumes and productivity have increased (Swedish Board of Agriculture,

2015). However, rural and regional development policies, partly linked to Sweden's EU membership, are bringing change and the emergence of a 'new Swedish rurality', characterized by farm diversification, increasing part-time farming, appreciation of quality food and expanding rural tourism and local food (Rytkönen, 2014). The organic food movement emerged in the 1980s from recognition of escalating environmental problems and heightened food quality concerns. An important organic actor in Sweden is KRAV (founded 1985), which sets standards that go beyond EU organic regulations, especially in terms of energy efficiency, animal welfare and workers' rights (KRAV, 2016).

In 2006, a policy stating that at least 20% of Sweden's agricultural land should be certified organic by the end of 2010 was introduced (Ministry of the Environment and Energy, 2006). This target was not met and overarching political targets for organic production or consumption are currently lacking (Ekologiskt forum, 2014). In 2013, the share of organic land and land under conversion was 16.5% (Swedish Board of Agriculture, 2014), which is the second highest proportion in the EU (Willer & Schaack, 2015). The market share of organic food products was 7.7% in 2015, after two years of significant growth: 39% in 2015 (Ekoweb, 2016) and 38% in 2014 (Ekoweb, 2015). Growing demand for organic produce has led to shortages (2015). The organic movement in Sweden has consistently aimed for united action (using the KRAV label), linking up with retailers rather than developing separate organic systems for processing and marketing (cf. Ekologiskt forum, 2014). Apart from farmers' markets and internet-based alternatives, fully organic food networks are rare. Consequently, large-scale retailers dominate, with three major retail chains accounting for over half of organic food sales (Ekoweb, 2015).

Methodology

The present analysis is based on empirical case studies on two organic food initiatives in Sweden: Ekolådan (EL) and Upplandsbondens (UB). A full account of the two cases can be found in Milestad and von Oelreich (2015a, 2015b).

EL is a KRAV-certified fruit and vegetable box scheme run by the non-profit foundation Biodynamic Products[1] (BP), based 40 km south-west of Stockholm. BP is the overarching business and decision-making unit. EL was launched as a project within BP and delivered its first boxes in autumn 2003, to its target group consisting primarily of households in the Stockholm region (Ekolådan, 2014). In the BP/EL food network, farmers deliver fruit and vegetables to the BP wholesaler and EL buys some of these for its boxes. Thus, BP/EL has sole control over the whole post-production network. Apart from EL, BP comprises three parts: a wholesaler, a trading company and two production units.

UB is a farmer-owned cooperative established in 2006. It has approximately 100 members, all KRAV-certified meat producers in Uppland province north of Stockholm. UB has no employees, but certain members have salaried positions on the board. Its main objective is to offer its members the best possible price for organic meat and ideally to sell it under its own brand, 'UB'. It seeks to keep meat production, processing and consumption within the region and only such meat products can be labelled UB. UB negotiates prices and seeks market solutions for its members. It also cooperates with a number of KRAV-certified farmers in mid-north Sweden, bringing their products to market. The overall UB food network comprises farmers, the UB cooperative (where only farmers are members), slaughterhouses, meat wholesalers, retailers and consumers. The largest volumes of meat are channelled via a national meat wholesaler to supermarkets throughout Sweden under a large retailer's own organic brand, and thus this meat cannot be identified as UB meat. A smaller volume is processed in cooperation with a local meat processor and sold in Uppland only. This meat carries the UB label. However, cooperation with the local processor has been compromised by diverging ideas on the importance of organic production. Limited volumes of UB meat are sold directly to consumers in meat-boxes, to a restaurant wholesaler or through public procurement processes.

Our research, conducted in 2014–2015, mainly consisted of semi-structured interviews (Kvale, 1996) with central respondents within EL and UB, together with analysis of key documents and websites. We conducted 15 interviews with 9 respondents holding key positions. The five respondents from BP/EL worked as: project developer for EL and chair of BP's board (abbreviated EL1); newsletter writer and former quality manager (EL2); senior purchaser (EL3); farmer delivering to BP/EL (EL4); and customer service manager (EL5). The four respondents from UB were: co-founder, farmer and treasurer of UB (UB1); CEO of UB's local processor partner (UB2); and co-founders and farmers (two respondents, UB3 and UB4). Having identified one important respondent for each case study, we used a snowball sampling technique to identify further interviewees (Biernacki & Waldorf, 1981), whereby the two central respondents were asked to identify other possible respondents, including people who might present contrasting information. This, in combination with repeated interviews with EL1, UB1 and EL4, allowed iterations and gave a rich picture of each initiative.

An interview guide was developed, covering questions on the organization, aims, development and history of each case, and issues relating to the overall food system. Eleven of the 15 interviews were held in person and 4 over the phone. Follow-up questions were asked by e-mail or over the telephone. All but two interviews were held in 2014, recorded and fully transcribed. The last two interviews were carried out in March 2015, at UB's annual meeting, where we took notes.

We analysed the empirical material collected in interviews and documents for the presence of main features of the food regime/food movement trends suggested by Holt Giménez and Shattuck (2011) (see Figure 1). To explore what food regime/food movement trends the studied initiatives can be attributed to, our analysis considered the basic orientation of the initiatives, the beneficiaries, the geographical scope, the solutions they provide and the types of food they advocate. To assess their transformational potential, the initiatives were analysed in terms of key ways in which niches can influence a regime, that is, growth, replication, learning and questioning the regime (Seyfang & Haxeltine, 2012).

Results from the case studies

Ekolådan

EL experienced a process of initial growth in 2003–2009, followed by decline and stabilization. It supplied 4500 home-delivered boxes per week at its peak before rapidly declining to half that level, for three reasons: (i) some customers could not afford to continue buying boxes after the economic crisis 2008/2009; (ii) improvements in the range of organic produce in mainstream supermarkets and (iii) increased competition from other home-delivery initiatives. The number of boxes has stabilized at around 2600/week (2015). Turnover rose from 7.4 to 25.5 million SEK/year between 2005 and 2014, with a peak of 33 million SEK in 2008. Thus, EL has not grown in pace with the overall organic market in Sweden.

In the 1990s, before EL was launched, BP was the only available supplier of organic food for a large mainstream retailer. However, as soon as the retailer developed its own organization and supply network, it ended its contract with BP. Practices pioneered by BP were thereby transferred into the mainstream regime, while BP moved on to a new niche:

> We pioneered organic meat ... we were the first to pack [organic] vegetables to all wholesalers in Sweden ... this is the way it has been with lots of things all the time, we pioneered organic bananas ... then the big ones come and push [us away] and then you have to move forward ... (EL1)

When EL proved successful, many other box schemes replicated its home-delivery model. However, most of the boxes in these schemes supply consumers with ingredients for predetermined dinners or their own choice of produce. EL decided not to follow this path, instead cultivating its direct relationship with farmers and letting availability decide the content of its boxes:

> A lot of trends emerged all the time and we looked at our competitors: 'Wow, they have dinner bags too, wow they have a raw food bag, they have a green drinks box', and this is when I felt 'no, this is not my thing ... I want fresh produce ...' We wanted to keep the possibility to plan with our growers. (EL2)

EL seeks to control its own chain, from producer to consumer, and to guarantee full transparency along the entire chain. Customers receive a newsletter with every box, listing the farmer and farm location for all delivered produce and raising awareness on issues such as agroecology, sustainable food systems, environmental protection and concentration of agri-food power. Thus, the newsletter is partly used to question the corporate food regime. EL boxes contain only organic produce. While relying on niche market certification (BP is a KRAV-certified business), EL does not put organic or other labels on its boxes, aiming for independence from mainstream tools such as certification:

> We have never wanted to bind ourselves to any label. For us as a specialist dealer, labelling has lost its significance since both KRAV and the Fairtrade label, oh – even worse – have actually become labels for the conventional industry. Then a small cutting edge enterprise like us, why should we have the same label as Chiquita? Dole Fruit, Philip Morris, whatever they are called, they all have these labels, so why should we have them? That gives us no profile. (EL1)

The non-profit foundation structure of BP/EL is a rare business model in Sweden. Its main goals are to avoid speculation and strive for long-term thinking (EL1). BP has built and maintains control over an independent food chain all the way from long-term farmer partners, via the BP wholesaler and distribution, to direct delivery to consumers' doors. Customers buy boxes directly from EL, without intermediaries. Thus, BP and EL have fully 'opted out' of the retail system and use their own supply chain where possible. For example, BP has established direct contact with banana farmers: '[BP/EL is] the only customer for 350 small-scale banana farmers in the Dominican Republic and that is a gigantic responsibility' (EL1). BP/EL is committed to buying from these farmers over the longer term, as a practical way of supporting sustainable livelihoods. There is awareness within EL of the power of major retailers and wholesalers and the increasingly fierce competition from retailers as they have expanded their organic ranges. However, expanding access to organic products is considered positive, since it develops the organic market overall and is in line with BP's aims to support organic farmers.

State support for organic farming was crucial for the emergence of EL. Thus, a solution used by the mainstream agriculture sector was also used by EL: 'That we could create Ekolådan in the first place built upon something quite historic – we received half the project budget [from the EU via the Swedish Board of Agriculture]' (EL1).

The BP foundation provided financial support for EL until it turned a profit. The foundation has launched several non-profit initiatives, for example, an apple farm: 'We have this apple farm ... that we try to save ... crazy in terms of profitability but enormously important culturally and ecologically, for [the foundation's] paragraph 1' (EL1). Pursuing ideologically motivated projects without the prospect of profits goes beyond mere business considerations.

EL strives to introduce social solutions to the food system, by 'providing consumers with organic and biodynamic food of high quality, in a way that gives growers the possibility to continue to develop' (Ekolådan, 2014). Its parent, BP, aims to 'support biodynamic/organic farmers by making their products easily available to all consumers, so that the farmers get a market and a serious and long-term partner' (Stiftelsen Biodynamiska Produkter, 2014). Thus, EL promotes high-quality organic food and highlights 'freshness' and 'quality' (EL1), 'fairness' (EL2), and connectedness between farmers and consumers. It aims for authenticity by including the names of growers in the newsletter accompanying each box. It also aims at enhancing the quality of food in its boxes through a high level of associated 'service and simplicity' (EL1) to customers, not least in terms of home delivery and a responsive customer service (EL5). EL's approach to quality relates to the 'high-end' segment of the market.

EL engages in trade beyond the local level, especially in fruit, but is committed to a local food systems model whenever possible. Our interviewees emphasized that farmers in both the Global North and the South should benefit from BP/EL operations. In terms of farmer benefit, EL is prepared to pre-finance farmers' production, facilitating their planning (EL3). Moreover, it pays farmers slightly above the reference prices for fruits and vegetables in Sweden (EL1). The senior purchaser of BP/EL seeks mutual benefit: 'It is not a combat, I try to work with trust, so that [farmers] do not exploit me, or the opposite' (EL3). Furthermore, 'I think in the long run getting the lowest possible price is not beneficial, it does not really work. Then [farmers] go to someone else and I have no security, so I might have no onions' (EL3). However, the farmer interviewed argued that prices do not cover the extra costs involved in biodynamic farming: 'in fact it is an almost impossible situation since we never get the price that we would need considering the concept we have when we farm biodynamically' (EL4).

In conclusion, BP/EL follows an alternative approach and aims at controlling its own food chain, from producer to consumer, setting the initiative apart from the wider organic niche and the overall regime.

Upplandsbondens

UB reflects the trend of increasing organic sales in Sweden. It has grown from 11 to 107 members (2014), with most organic meat farmers in Uppland being members. Turnover rose from about 2 to over 24 million SEK/year between 2007 and 2013. However, UB has experienced significant obstacles in reaching consumers with its own local brand. The main challenge has been finding suitable partners sharing UB's values and willing to use the UB label. Its local processor partner introduced UB's KRAV-certified products into its range not through sharing UB's commitment to Organic 3.0, but rather for pure market considerations: '[Marketing] conventional meat in combination with a KRAV-labelled range … is a significant advantage. We are much stronger as an actor on the market if we have both conventional and KRAV [products]' (UB2).

UB cooperates with a large mainstream wholesaler, through which it sells around 80% of its meat. Together with its partners in mid-north Sweden, UB has shown that scaling up has a tangible impact on the mainstream food system. The volumes of organic meat it provides to its wholesaler partner have increased the amount of organic meat available to consumers at retail. UB's national wholesaler partner requires delivery of at least 1000 animals per year and puts pressure on UB to increase this number, which decreases UB's possibilities to develop its independent brand. UB faces a conflict between delivering enough to its wholesaler partner and keeping enough animals to sell under its own label:

> We cannot promise [our partner] more than 1000 to 1200 of our 2000 animals and they think this is bordering on too little … They tell us 'well, [if you cannot deliver] then we will buy animals from other producers … ' (UB1)

Thus, UB tries to balance supplying the retailer with large volumes of meat and developing its own label, which decreases dependence on one wholesaler:

> We have always had the principle that we should not end up in the lap of [our wholesaler partner], that is very risky. We need an independent brand … [Our aim is to] … create demand for our label … otherwise we are totally doomed. (UB1)

However, UB does not want to control its own food network, but prefers to specialize in primary production and collaborate with suitable market partners. Initial ideas about setting up an independent organic store selling members' products were abandoned due to lack of resources and capacity; 'none of us farmers could cope with it, it would take an incredible amount of work' (UB1).

UB initially spread knowledge about organic production through cooperation with its partner wholesaler. When that partner ventured into the organic niche, it had no expertise of its own on organic meat, but UB helped to educate key people within the wholesaler in handling organic meat; 'We taught them everything about KRAV, they did not know anything about KRAV and organics before' (UB1).

UB goes beyond EU organic regulations in being KRAV-certified. UB rests on KRAV-certified production, animal welfare and landscape stewardship through grazing natural pastures. These aspects are highly valued by UB members and are important elements of its profile beyond Organic 2.0:

> Our philosophy has always been that what binds the farmers to Upplandsbondens is ... the interest in creating an independent brand and the joy in seeing your animals treated well. This has been decisive for farmers joining Upplandsbondens. (UB1)

UB strongly promotes certification of its niche, in terms of both its regional organic label (UB) and the national organic label (KRAV).

While UB has quite weak links to wider food movements, it is connected to the farm cooperative movement in Sweden. Most UB members are members of the organic farmers' association and many are organic pioneers. As an organization, UB is controlled through a cooperative structure. Everyone has one vote at the annual assembly. Cooperatives are a common organizational form for farmers in Sweden:

> Traditionally we have used cooperatives among farmers and I think it is an unbelievably good form of association to engage in ... We thought this was the best form, I think it is difficult with a company, there profits rule, here returning the most pay to the farmer is our main idea. (UB3)

However, values have sometimes been strained within the association, notably between those few members who want higher prices (which can be obtained through slaughter outside the region) and the majority for whom this would be unthinkable.

UB farmer interviewees emphasized the importance of solidarity with local farmers, since buying local products also benefits the wider rural community through feedback loops to local employment: 'If Swedish farmers cannot sell [their organic products], if they do not get a good price, they will not buy any equipment, they will not buy any spare parts, and then you have no jobs ... everything is connected' (UB3). As an organization, UB networks with businesses such as restaurants, but also with other food actors, and some UB farmers have a long history of launching various organic food initiatives and of participating in farmers' markets.

In its early years, UB relied on state support from the EU, via the Swedish Board of Agriculture, which was decisive for its marketing endeavours. UB farmers' lack of resources and limited margins prevented them from investing in marketing and developing their own brand without state support:

> That is a constant problem for farmers; bad economic conditions. Not many farms have the resources ... we had too narrow margins and [without support] we could only have reached half-way ... Thanks to the 'value-added support' from the Swedish Board of Agriculture, well the EU, we were able to invest money in [marketing], which was critical since it costs money to create a brand. (UB1)

The kind of food UB produces can be classified as 'high-quality food', sold primarily to consumers prepared to pay a premium for organic meat. UB meat is also sold as a high-end 'buy local' product to high-end restaurants in Stockholm. UB also focuses on meat quality and flavour and rearing animals on natural pastures:

> When you buy meat from Upplandsbondens you get a tasty, high-quality meat, where the spice is the grass and herbs growing naturally, grazed in our beautiful landscape. The only additive we use is care for our animals. In summer our animals live and graze freely. In winter they often range outdoors, while having access to shelter from wind and rain. They have free access to hay or fodder made from grass and clover. (Upplandsbondens, 2016)

In terms of geographical focus, UB is committed to local production and a locally oriented food system, where production and consumption take place within its geographical region.

However, due to UB's dependence on mainstreaming, its local food system aspirations are only partly fulfilled in practice, as UB meat is sold all over Sweden. Thus, the intention to keep production, slaughter, distribution and consumption fully within the region has not been achieved, since some slaughter is done outside the region and since the bulk of the meat is sold beyond the region.

In summary, UB has achieved substantial growth through mainstreaming its products, securing benefits for its farmer members, while struggling to promote its own Organic 3.0 label.

Discussion

A transformational shift in the global food system is beyond the scope of individual food initiatives (Holt Giménez & Shattuck, 2011), and requires political action (Scoones, Newell, & Leach, 2015). However, individual organic initiatives can contribute to change by pushing the organic niche and the overall food system towards sustainability transformations through demonstrating viable ways forward. The two food initiatives studied here share key characteristics in their relations with the corporate food regime, but also differ in important respects.

EL and UB operate in a food systems context where environmental landscape pressures are rising (cf. Marsden, 2013; Rockström & Karlberg, 2010). Both are alternatives to the dominant regime, spurring social innovation, but in different ways: EL has built a separate system based on social concerns all the way from producer to consumer, while UB farmers pioneered organic meat production in their region and the cooperative has managed to improve prices, and thus social conditions, for its members.

EL and its parent BP follow a progressive and partly radical approach and have kept their values over time. BP expresses its progressive approach through supporting organic growers, while EL has consistently followed an alternative 'separate niche' model. Although BP once tried to expand through mainstreaming, it has abandoned this approach. Being a foundation has facilitated investment in innovative projects, and BP has helped EL to retain its ideals. EL's focus on quality food has helped it to reach urban 'high-end' consumers, but it aims to introduce these consumers to Organic 3.0 food, demonstrating its progressive intentions. BP/EL questions both mainstream organic labels and the corporate food regime.

UB mainly follows a reformist approach based on mainstreaming, but with some progressive and radical traits relating to its ambitions for local production and consumption and its focus on solidarity within the cooperative, notably by securing the best possible price for its members. It could be argued that in trying simultaneously to follow reformist and (their preferred) progressive approaches, UB farmers have had to partly compromise their own values to reach profitability. Market possibilities push UB towards reformism, which is more profitable. Both dominant market actors and smaller partners to UB are conventional businesses and, in cooperating with such partners, the reformist logic limits UB's progressive and radical ambitions. However, UB has also actively chosen a reformist approach in terms of mainstreaming. It adheres to the idea that sustainably produced organic food should be found in ordinary supermarkets, to reach all consumers in society, which could be considered a progressive stance. This explains UB's reformist approach, since building a separate food network would counteract its aim to mainstream into food chains already in place. Thus, UB can be said to apply a mainstreaming approach to achieve a progressive aim.

Although the food regime/food movements framework suggested by Holt Giménez and Shattuck (2011) provides analytical clarity and paints an overarching picture of the global food system and its contestations, its simplified representation of the system obscures some of the complexities involved. In one sense, alternatives such as EL and UB exist within the realm of the corporate food regime, regardless of their specific orientation, since they have to relate to the regime and its power relations and since the contradiction they express through building alternatives to the regime intrinsically links them to it (Bernstein, 2015). In another sense, EL and UB fall within the corporate food regime only when expressing neoliberal or purely reformist traits. EL and UB can be positioned beyond the corporate food regime, not because they are 'separate, autonomous or somehow autarchic, but in order to assess their potential to influence the regime' (Holt Giménez & Shattuck, 2011, p. 116). Furthermore, they can be positioned beyond the neoliberal trend, since they follow fully organic approaches and pursue social and environmental aims beyond profit. Making a distinction between EL and UB, on the one hand, and the corporate food regime in general and the neoliberal trend in particular, on the other, is illuminating. However, it is important to avoid oversimplification and recognize the hybridity of actual food initiatives. Both EL and UB show traits of several food system trends, but UB provides the clearest example of hybridity in straddling the reformist–progressive divide, showing that organic initiatives cannot be ascribed solely to one trend in the food system (cf. Holt Giménez & Shattuck, 2011).

Through their emphasis on a wider understanding of organic food, both EL and UB approach Organic 3.0, which overlaps with the progressive and radical trends in the food system (cf. Gould, 2015; Holt Giménez & Shattuck, 2011). From this perspective, they can be seen as part of a 'niche within the niche' of organic food production in Sweden. As pointed out by Marsden, 'social and governance innovation' in food system niches challenging the mainstream 'may be crucial for regime change' (2013, p. 124). In addition to innovativeness, in order to succeed, transitional processes also need to result in 'persistent' niche creation (van der Ploeg et al., 2004, p. 10). This raises the question of what EL and UB have contributed to enduring Organic 3.0 niche creation.

Niche impact on the regime can take the form of niche growth, replication, learning and questioning the regime (Seyfang & Haxeltine, 2012). Regarding niche growth, the trajectories of EL and UB differ. The approach based on mainstreaming used by UB has facilitated its growth, while EL's separate system approach has limited its growth, but questions the regime and represents an innovative alternative model. UB has significantly influenced supply by offering large volumes of organic meat to its mainstream retail partners, thus expanding consumer access to organic products. However, this has partly compromised the Organic 3.0 identity of UB meat, since those products are sold without the UB label. Thus, regime influence on UB outweighs UB's influence on the regime and the extent to which UB has managed to sustain its 'niche within a niche' can be questioned, despite its intentions. Although UB's operations are not marginalized by the mainstream (cf. Marsden, 2013), its 'niche within a niche' existence is partly unaccomplished. Regime shift requires persistent niche development, so the transformational impact of UB to date can be seen as limited. EL, on the other hand, has managed to consolidate its 'niche within a niche' existence, but on a modest scale and with no growth during the second half of its existence.

In the context of organic food and farming, Allen and Kovach conclude that 'Fundamental change ... is not likely to occur through the market alone' (2000, p. 221). Thus, the potential influence of EL and UB on the corporate food regime is wider than their direct market impact. The primary role of Organic 3.0 initiatives may be to illustrate the viability of alternative models, since the 'true measure of these alternatives might be the inspiration they give to others to envision an alternate way of being in the food system' (Hendrickson & Heffernan, 2002, p. 366). As models of inspiration, EL and UB might induce food systems change through replication (Seyfang & Haxeltine, 2012). EL has significant potential for niche influence through replication, as few Organic 3.0 box schemes exist in Sweden. An emergence of multiple organic box schemes, together influencing the regime, might be preferable to growth of a single scheme. In this regard, BP has acted as a forerunner, pioneering alternative business models and projects (including EL).

For UB, replication has taken the form of incorporating farmers in mid-north Sweden under its umbrella, simultaneously amounting to a scale-up of operations. However, production growth has been swallowed by mainstream organic, preventing Organic 3.0 values being realized. As proposed by Elzen et al. (2012), the degree of linking and 'anchoring' of innovative practices helps to explain niche impact on the regime: EL has managed to anchor home-delivery boxes into the regime, but its Organic 3.0 values have not followed, while UB has managed to link strongly to the regime by delivering large amounts of organic meat into the mainstream, but Organic 3.0 values are hidden on the way. To anchor, or more robustly link, innovative social and sustainable practices with the regime, EL would need to grow or spur the development of initiatives sharing similar values, while UB would need to sell its products under its own Organic 3.0 label.

Both EL and UB have had an impact on the organic niche and the food regime. Although limited in scale, EL represents an alternative approach, questioning both Organic 2.0 and the regime. Through its growth, UB has widened consumer access to organic products, but translation of Organic 3.0 values into the wider organic niche and the regime has been limited. Thus, linking Organic 3.0 values to the wider niche and the overarching regime remains a challenge. In the case of EL, its separate system approach does not link up with the niche or regime. In the case of UB, while promoting organic production, its Organic 3.0 values are masked by interaction with the mainstream. Further research is needed on how different niche strategies can be combined to achieve the transformational aim of Organic 3.0 becoming 'the mainstream choice for agriculture [...] but also its leading edge' (Gould, 2015, p. 137). Such transformation will require persistent 'niche within a niche' creation (cf. van der Ploeg et al., 2004), building Organic 3.0 values and translating them into the organic niche and the wider regime.

Conclusions: enlarging the space for Organic 3.0

This study departs from the assumption that individual Organic 3.0 food initiatives, as a 'niche within the organic niche', may differ in their potential to influence the corporate food regime and that this potential can be assessed by examining traits linked to reformist, progressive or radical food regime/food movement trends that they possess. Rather than implying a simplistic dichotomy between niche and food regime or categorizing initiatives with reformist, progressive or radical trends, we explored the nuances, complexities, hybridities and overlaps in niche–regime relationships within the food system from an MLP.

Organic 3.0 initiatives differ from each other, as illustrated here through application of the framework suggested by Holt Giménez and Shattuck (2011). However, that framework does not describe how initiatives influence the wider organic niche or the corporate food regime. As explained by the MLP, social innovation (Marsden, 2013) and persistence are key to long-term niche creation (van der Ploeg et al., 2004). Persistent pursuit of Organic 3.0 and its novel interpretation of sustainability is required to build a solid sub-niche that can push the wider organic niche and the overall food system towards sustainability transformations. Although individual Organic 3.0 initiatives can influence the organic niche and the overarching regime, it is difficult to assess their overall influence on the regime. Nevertheless, from a sustainability transformations perspective, even small-scale change is valuable. No individual initiative can shift the regime, but 'alternative movements should not be overlooked for their real work of protecting existing spaces of action or for creating or enlarging those spaces' (Hendrickson & Heffernan, 2002, p. 366).

Organic practices are collective. In aiming for sustainability transformations, initiatives such as EL and UB need to work with partners that share their values and forge 'strategic alliances' with other actors in the food system (Holt Giménez & Shattuck, 2011, p. 136). Moving towards Organic 3.0 will involve maintaining and deepening the qualitative edge of organic, while at the same time translating innovative social practices and values into the mainstream. This poses a considerable challenge, not least since edge and mainstream are often at odds, as shown in this paper. Further research is needed on the potential of a transformed, and broadly sustainability-oriented organic movement to organize, grow and flourish in the gaps of the corporate food regime, while gradually advancing in the direction of regime shift.

Note

1. Stiftelsen biodynamiska produkter, in Swedish.

Acknowledgements

We thank two anonymous reviewers for valuable comments.

Disclosure statement

No potential conflict of interest was reported by the authors.

Funding

This work was supported by Forskningsrådet Formas (Swedish Research Council Formas) being a partner of the FP7 ERA-net project CORE Organic II [grant number 2012-1937].

ORCID

Jacob von Oelreich http://orcid.org/0000-0002-3722-6084
Rebecka Milestad http://orcid.org/0000-0002-8626-7288

References

Allen, P., & Kovach, M. (2000). The capitalist composition of organic: The potential of markets in fulfilling the promise of organic agriculture. *Agriculture and Human Values, 17*, 221–232. doi:10.1023/A:1007640506965

Arbenz, M., Gould, D., & Stopes, C. (2015). *Organic 3.0: For truly sustainable farming & consumption* (Discussion Paper). Retrieved from IFOAM-Organics International: http://www.ifoam.bio/sites/default/files/organic_3.0_discussion_paper.pdf

Bernstein, H. (2015, June). *Food regimes and food regime analysis: A selective survey*. Paper presented at the conference land grabbing, conflict and agrarian-environmental transformations: Perspectives from East and Southeast Asia, Chiang Mai University, Chiang Mai.

Biernacki, P., & Waldorf, D. (1981). Snowball sampling: Problems and techniques of chain referral sampling. *Sociological Methods Research, 10*, 141–163. doi:10.1177/004912418101000205

Bui, S., Cardona, A., Lamine, C., & Cerf, M. (2016). Sustainability transitions: Insights on processes of niche–regime interaction and regime reconfiguration in agri-food systems. *Journal of Rural Studies, 48*, 92–103. doi:10.1016/j.jrurstud.2016.10.003

Dantsi, T., Loumou, A., & Giourga, C. (2009). Organic agriculture's approach towards sustainability: Its relationship with the agro-industrial complex: A case study in Central Macedonia, Greece. *Journal of Agricultural and Environmental Ethics, 22*, 197–216. doi:10.1007/s10806-008-9139-0

Darnhofer, I. (2015). Socio-technical transitions in farming: Key concepts. In L.-A. Sutherland, I. Darnhofer, G. A. Wilson, & L. Zagata (Eds.), *Transition pathways towards sustainability in agriculture: Case studies from Europe* (pp. 17–32). Wallingford, CT: CABI.

Davidson, D. J., Jones, K. E., & Parkins, J. R. (2016). Food safety risks, disruptive events and alternative beef production: A case study of agricultural transition in Alberta. *Agriculture and Human Values, 33*, 359–371. doi:10.1007/s10460-015-9609-8

Ekolådan. (2014). *Ekolådans rötter* [The roots of Ekolådan]. Retrieved from www.ekoladan.se

Ekologiskt forum. (2014). *Samling ger eko! En strategi för ökad ekologisk konsumtion och produktion* [Strategy for increased organic consumption and production]. Retrieved from http://ekologisktforum.se/wp-content/uploads/2011/05/Ekologiskt-Forum-2014.pdf

Ekoweb. (2015). *Ekologisk livsmedelsmarknad: Rapport om den ekologiska branschen sammanställd av Ekoweb.nu* [Report on the organic sector compiled by Ekoweb.nu]. Retrieved from http://www.ekoweb.nu/attachments/67/27.pdf

Ekoweb. (2016). *Ekologisk livsmedelsmarknad: Rapport om den ekologiska branschen sammanställd av Ekoweb.nu* [Report on the organic sector compiled by Ekoweb.nu]. Retrieved from http://www.e-pages.dk/maskinbladet/1180/

Elzen, B., van Mierlo, B., & Leeuwis, C. (2012). Anchoring of innovations: Assessing Dutch efforts to harvest energy from glasshouses. *Environmental Innovation and Societal Transitions, 5*, 1–18. doi:10.1016/j.eist.2012.10.006

Friedmann, H. (1993). The political economy of food: A global crisis. *New Left Review, 197*, 29–57.

Geels, F. W. (2010). Ontologies, socio-technical transitions (to sustainability), and the multi-level perspective. *Research Policy, 39*, 495–510. doi:10.1016/j.respol.2010.01.022

Geels, F. W. (2011). The multi-level perspective on sustainability transitions: Responses to seven criticisms. *Environmental Innovation and Societal Transitions, 1*, 24–40. doi:10.1016/j.eist.2011.02.002

Goldberger, J. R. (2011). Conventionalization, civic engagement, and the sustainability of organic agriculture. *Journal of Rural Studies, 27*, 288–296. doi:10.1016/j.jrurstud.2011.03.002

Gould, D. (2015). The organic market framework: Becoming Organic 3.0. In H. Willer, & J. Lernoud (Eds.), *The world of organic agriculture: Statistics and emerging trends 2015* (Report) (pp. 137–140). Frick: Research Institute of Organic Agriculture (FiBL) & Bonn: IFOAM – Organics International.

Hendrickson, M. K., & Heffernan, W. D. (2002). Opening spaces through relocalization: Locating potential resistance in the weaknesses of the global food system. *Sociologia Ruralis, 42*(4), 347–369. doi:10.1111/1467-9523.00221

Hinrichs, C. C. (2014). Transitions to sustainability: A change in thinking about food systems change? *Agriculture and Human Values, 31*, 143–155. doi:10.1007/s10460-014-9479-5

Holt Giménez, E., & Shattuck, A. (2011). Food crises, food regimes and food movements: Rumblings of reform or tides of transformation? *Journal of Peasant Studies, 38*(1), 109–144. doi:10.1080/03066150.2010.538578

IAASTD. (2008). *International assessment of agricultural knowledge, science and technology for development: Executive summary of the synthesis report* (Report). Washington, DC: Island Press.

KRAV. (2016). *Regler för KRAV-certifierad produktion utgåva 2016* [Rules for KRAV certified production edition 2016]. Uppsala: KRAV Ekonomisk förening.

Kvale, S. (1996). *Interviews: An introduction to qualitative research interviewing*. Thousand Oaks, CA: SAGE.

Marsden, T. (2013). From post-productionism to reflexive governance: Contested transitions in securing more sustainable food futures. *Journal of Rural Studies, 29*, 123–134. doi:10.1016/j.jrurstud.2011.10.001

McMichael, P. (2014). *Food regimes and agrarian questions: Agrarian change & peasant studies*. Rugby: PracticalAction.

Milestad, R., & von Oelreich, J. (2015a). *Full case study report: Ekolådan – Sweden* (HealthyGrowth Report). Stockholm: KTH Royal Institute of Technology. Retrieved from http://orgprints.org/29251

Milestad, R., & von Oelreich, J. (2015b). *Full case study report: Upplandsbondens – Sweden* (HealthyGrowth Report). Stockholm: KTH Royal Institute of Technology. Retrieved from http://orgprints.org/29250

Ministry of the Environment and Energy. (2006). *Ekologisk produktion och konsumtion: Mål och inriktning till 2010. Skr. 2005/06:88* [Organic production and consumption: Goals and orientation until 2010. Communication 2005/06:88] (Government Policy). Retrieved from http://www.regeringen.se/rattsdokument/skrivelse/2006/03/skr.-20050688/

Olsson, P., Galaz, V., & Boonstra, W. J. (2014). Sustainability transformations: A resilience perspective. *Ecology and Society, 19*(4), 1. doi:10.5751/ES-06799-190401

van der Ploeg, J. D., Bouma, J., Rip, A., Rijkenberg, F. H. J., Ventura, F., & Wiskerke, J. S. C. (2004). On regimes, novelties, niches and co-production. In J. S. C. Wiskerke & J. D. van der Ploeg (Eds.), *Seeds of transition: Essays on novelty production, niches and regimes in agriculture* (pp. 1–30). Assen: Royal Van Gorcum.

Raskin, P., Banuri, T., Gallopin, G., Gutman, P., Hammond, A., Kates, R., & Swart, R. (2002). *Great transition: The promise and lure of the times ahead* (Report of the Global Scenario Group). Boston, MA: Stockholm Environment Institute & Tellus Institute.

Rockström, J., & Karlberg, L. (2010). The quadruple squeeze: Defining the safe operating space for freshwater use to achieve a triply green revolution in the Anthropocene. *Ambio, 39*(3), 257–265. doi:10.1007/s13280-010-0033-4

Rosin, C., & Campbell, H. (2009). Beyond bifurcation: Examining the conventions of organic agriculture in New Zealand. *Journal of Rural Studies, 25*, 35–47. doi:10.1016/j.jrurstud.2008.05.002

Rytkönen, P. (2014). Constructing the new rurality: Challenges and opportunities of a recent shift in Swedish rural policies. In T. Aenis, A. Knierim, M.-C. Riecher, R. Ridder, H. Schobert, & H. Fischer (Eds.), *Farming systems facing global challenges: Capacities and strategies* (pp. 1195–1205). Vienna: Boku University & IFSA.

Schewe, R. L. (2014). Letting go of 'Conventionalisation': Family labour on New Zealand organic dairy farms. *Sociologia Ruralis, 55*(1), 85–105. doi:10.1111/soru.12066

Seyfang, G., & Haxeltine, A. (2012). Growing grassroots innovations: Exploring the role of community-based initiatives in governing sustainable energy transitions. *Environment and Planning C: Government and Policy, 30*, 381–400. Retrieved from http://journals.sagepub.com/doi/abs/10.1068/c10222

Seyfang, G., & Smith, A. (2007). Grassroots innovations for sustainable development: Towards a new research and policy agenda. *Environmental Politics, 16*, 584–603. doi:10.1080/09644010701419121

Scoones, I., Newell, P., & Leach, M. (2015). The politics of green transformations. In I. Scoones, M. Leach, & P. Newell (Eds.), *The politics of green transformations* (pp. 1–24). Abingdon: Routledge.

Stiftelsen Biodynamiska Produkter. (2014). *Vår filosofi* [Our philosophy]. Retrieved from http://www.biodynamiskaprodukter.se

Swedish Board of Agriculture. (2014). *Jordbruksstatistisk årsbok 2014* [Yearbook of agricultural statistics]. Retrieved from www.jordbruksverket.se

Swedish Board of Agriculture. (2015). *Basfakta om svenskt jordbruk* [Basic facts on Swedish agriculture]. Retrieved from https://www.jordbruksverket.se/amnesomraden/konsument/faktaochrapporter/basfaktaomsvensktjordbruk.4.5125de613acf69a0f680001878.html

Upplandsbondens. (2016). *Ekologiskt kött med smak av den uppländska naturen* [Organic meat with a taste of Uppland's nature]. Retrieved from www.upplandsbondens.se

Willer, H., & Schaack, D. (2015). Organic farming and market development in Europe. In H. Willer & J. Lernoud (Eds.), *The world of organic agriculture: Statistics and emerging trends 2015* (pp. 181–214). Frick/Bonn: Research Institute of Organic Agriculture (FiBL)/IFOAM-Organics International.

How relationships can influence an organic firm's network identity

Gunn-Turid Kvam, Hilde Bjørkhaug and Ann-Charlott Pedersen

ABSTRACT
A main challenge when organic food actors cooperate with conventional food actors is to maintain their identity in the relationship. In this paper, we analyse such a relationship through the use of the industrial marketing and purchasing perspective (IMP). The aim is to increase knowledge about changes in relationships that occur through growth processes and about how new relationships influence the identity of a quality-oriented firm. We use a case-study method when examining the relationship between the organic Røros Dairy and the retail chain Coop, and its effects on relationships within the dairy network. Results show that the focal relationship influences, and in turn is influenced by, the dairy's network. Because of the dairy's strong identity that preceded its formal cooperation with Coop, as well as its reputation for quality production and continuous product development, the dairy has strengthened its position in the network. We conclude that the IMP perspective contributes a valuable framework in this study of an organic food network. For business managers, our results highlight the importance of considering possible effects of relationships on the identity one would want to convey.

Introduction

Research about strategies used in organic food chains has mainly focused on either mainstream, large-scale food chains or small-scale local marketing initiatives. Some challenges underlie these two strategies for selling organic produce. Large-scale players have a limited capacity or ability to transmit information about organic values beyond basic standards and regulations including those from the EU (Noe & Alrøe, 2011). As Guthman (2004) points out, large-scale organic food chains are becoming conventionalized and organic food is not differentiated markedly from other foods. The characteristics inherent in small-scale initiatives are a problem when moving from niche production to volume production (Mount, 2012). When the literature describes these two types of organic chains, there are fewer examples of organic mid-scale chains (Knutsen et al., 2006). The project Healthy Growth[1] has focused on organic food chains that have remained true to their roots and have avoided developing the mainstream conventional characteristics mentioned above, even as they grow. These chains, which we call 'mid-scale values-based organic chains', have succeeded in combining volume and organic and other values (Kvam & Bjørkhaug, 2014).

An aim of mid-scale values-based organic chains is to differentiate between conventional and organic conventionalized food chains when the lowest price is the focus. To differentiate, mid-scale chains add quality to products that demand a premium price to cover costs. The literature emphasizes organic chains and organic products that usually embody a range of added qualities such as local products, use of local recipes and local raw material, locally processed as well as qualities connected to rural development (for example, Marsden, Banks, & Bristow, 2000; Marsden & Smith, 2005). Research also emphasizes the establishment of new network relationships in such chains. These chains are often regional and embedded with close relationships and mutual trust between chain actors (Marsden & Smith, 2005; Marsden et al., 2000; Noe, 2007; Schermer, Matscher, & Borec, 2010; Schermer, Renting, & Ostindie, 2011; Stevenson, 2009). Research on U.S. mid-scale values-based organic chains highlights a close relationship between cooperating partners (Stevenson & Pirog, 2008). Successful value chains emphasize shared values and visions regarding product quality, partner relationships, customer treatment, and shared information (transparency) and shared decision-making among strategic partners (Stevenson, 2009).

The distinction between a conventional and an alternative food system, as found in the research literature, does not describe the situation among successful mid-scale values-based organic food chains. Instead, most enterprises employ hybrid solutions (Kvam & Bjørkhaug, 2014). Hybrid solutions are discussed in a range of research on local food systems (e.g. in Ilbery, Courtney, Kirwan, & Maye, 2010; Ostrom & Jussaume, 2007; Sonnino & Marsden, 2006). According to Mount (2012), an important question is whether growth brings into question the perception of hybridity and how growth can influence the perceived 'identity' of any system that constitutes itself as an alternative. The ability of a quality-oriented producer to deliver sometimes intangible qualities and to maintain a distinction as an alternative to conventional food systems is critical to gain any premium price for local food (Marsden et al., 2000). Thus, according to Mount (2012), growing organic chains must carefully consider how they can maintain an alternative identity within the context of hybridity.

In this paper, we use a case-study method for studying the relationship between a regional mid-scale organic firm and a conventional actor. Our objective is to examine the effects of this organic firm's relationship on its connected relationships and vice versa, and how the organic firm's relationship with a conventional actor affects the firm's identity as a regional organic actor. The study is intended to provide evidence about the complex network and business relations that are part of a scaling-up process. We use an industrial marketing and purchasing perspective (IMP) as our theoretical approach. Research questions for the study are outlined below.

(1) How does a focal relationship between a regional organic actor and a conventional actor influence connected relationships and vice versa?
(2) How does the focal relationship influence the regional actor's network identity?
(3) How is it possible to influence the development of one's own identity in the network?

(4) How can our study contribute to increased understanding of growth processes in organic chains?

The theoretical perspective is outlined below. We then present the methodology and the case of Røros Dairy and its network and analyse the network effects of relationships and on the network identity of the dairy. Finally, we discuss findings and conclude.

The industrial network perspective

IMP has been presented by, for example, Axelsson and Easton (1992), Håkansson and Snehota (1995), Ford et al. (1998), Ford, Gadde, Håkansson, and Snehota (2003) and Håkansson, Ford, Gadde, Snehota, and Waluszewski (2009). The IMP perspective describes and explains a range of inter-organizational phenomena such as marketing, purchasing, technical development and strategy, and has contributed significantly to our understanding of relationships between firms. The basic assumption is that a single firm is embedded in a network of other firms with which the focal firm (the firm studied) has substantial and continuous business relationships; these relationships are connected to each other. This connection implies that the actions of a single firm must be seen both in relation to the other firms in the network and in terms of the relationships between these firms (Anderson, Håkansson, & Johanson, 1994). This perspective is different from the resource-based perspective, which is the perspective of another theoretical school in this field, where the focus is on the sum of the resources a firm is able to mobilize for development (e.g. Barney, 1991; Wernerfelt, 1984). The IMP perspective focuses on development as part of a network structure that may both facilitate and limit development (Håkansson & Snehota, 1995).

Hence, business networks can be regarded in different ways. According to Miles and Snow (1992), business networks can be defined as sets of connected firms. Alternatively, Cook and Emerson (1978) and Anderson et al. (1994) characterize business networks as sets of connected relationships between firms. The latter definition reflects the IMP perspective's view on business networks. In their 2009 book, Håkansson et al. use the metaphor of the rainforest, indicating 'that the basic feature of the business landscape is the intricate interdependence between the companies that populate it' (p. 1). This definition is in contrast to the more traditional way of describing the business landscape as a jungle where hard competition is the rule.

To understand the issue of connected relationships, the IMP perspective has been inspired by research within the field of social exchange theory. Cook and Emerson discuss exchange networks as a set of two or more connected exchange relations. They define the concept of connection as follows:

> Two exchange relations are connected to the degree that exchange in one relation is contingent upon exchange (or nonexchange) in the other relation. The connection is positive if exchange in one is contingent upon exchange in the other. The connection is negative if exchange in one is contingent upon nonexchange in the other. (Cook & Emerson, 1978, p. 725)

Emerson (1972 [cited in Yamagishi, Gillmore, & Cook, 1988, p. 835]) has elaborated on what is meant by positive and negative connections claiming that

If two relations, A-B and B-C, are positively connected at B, exchanges in the A-B relation facilitate exchanges in the B-C relation and vice versa. If the same two relations are negatively connected at B, exchanges in the A-B relation diminish or prohibit exchanges in the B-C relation and vice versa.

Thus, when relationships are positively connected at B, B exchanges, for example, resources to C, which is a result of B's relationship to A. When relationships are negatively connected at B, this can imply that A and C are fighting over the same resources controlled by B.

Ritter (2000) further elaborated on the concept of connection when he discussed and analysed the interconnectedness of relationships. Using the definition by Cook and Emerson (1978), he discusses connections between firms A, B and C, and relationships x, y and z as illustrated in Figure 1.

According to Ritter (2000, p. 319),

the impact of one relationship (x) on another relationship (y) can have three different features: 1. Relationship (x) has no impact on relationship (y) ... 2. Relationship (x) has an overall positive impact on relationship (y); i.e. the existence of relationship (x) is supporting, enabling or even enforcing the existence of relationship (y) ... 3. Relationship (x) has an overall negative impact on relationship (y); i.e. the existence of relationship (x) is hindering, disabling or even excluding the existence of relationship (y).

Since this definition of interconnectedness implies that the connectedness goes both ways, two given relationships (x) and (y) will mutually affect each other but not necessary in the same way. Thus, Ritter (2000) has developed six different cases of interconnectedness between any two relationships which he labels as:

(1) neutrality effect (no interconnectedness between the two relationships)
(2) assistance effect (one-sided positive effect)
(3) hindrance effect (one-sided negative effect)
(4) synergy effect (two-way positive effect)
(5) lack effect (one-way positive and the other way negative effect)
(6) competition effect (two-way negative effect)

As Ritter (2000) pointed out, the time dimension is lacking in his cases, and analysis using the cases does not capture the dynamic dimension.

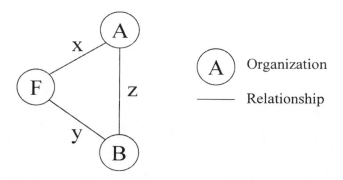

Figure 1. Connections between relationships. Source: Based on Ritter (2000, p. 320).

A single business relationship can exist in itself and, simultaneously, be embedded in a context through its connections with other relationships. Anderson et al. (1994) have distinguished between primary and secondary functions of a relationship. The primary function speaks to the positive and negative effects of interaction on the two parties in a focal relationship. The secondary function is also called the network function and focuses on the positive and negative effects of connected relationships. Anderson et al. (1994) discuss how to conceptualize business networks as sets of connected relationships, and use this conceptualization to develop the concept of network identity. To develop the network identity concept, they start by defining the concept of network horizon as 'how extended an actor's view of the network is' (Anderson et al., 1994, p. 4). Thus, the network horizon of a firm includes other firms and relationships of which the focal firm is aware. Furthermore, Anderson et al. (1994, p. 4) define the network context as follows: 'the part of the network within the horizon that the actor considers relevant is the actor's network context'. Thus, according to this view, the focal firm defines what is the useful context for a given relationship depending on how the focal firm perceives its network horizon. Holmen and Pedersen (2003, p. 411) have highlighted the difference between the two concepts by stating that 'the part of the network, which a single firm is aware of, is its network horizon. In addition, the part of the network horizon which the firm considers relevant is the firm's network context'.

Anderson et al. (1994, p. 4) base their discussion and definition of network identity on this notion of the business network when they claim

> Network identity is meant to capture the perceived attractiveness (or repulsiveness) of a firm as an exchange partner due to its unique set of connected relations with other firms … It refers to how firms see themselves in the network and how they are seen by other network actors.

Thus, to analyse the firm's network identity, we need to identify other firms and the relationships in the (focal) firm's network context. Hence, the identity of an actor is defined by what the actor represents to other specific actors with whom the actor is interacting (La Rocca, 2013).

Anderson et al. (1994, p. 6) have presented a framework for identifying positive and negative effects on the network identity.

Constructive (positive) effects on network identity can be classified in the resource, activity and actor dimensions in the following ways:

- Use of knowledge or solutions from other relationships and/or use of created knowledge or solutions in other relationships lead to resource transferability.
- Contingent positive volume effects and/or contingent positive qualitative effects lead to activity complementarity.
- Harmonious signalling to other relations and/or attractive connectedness of partners lead to actor-relation generalizability.

Similarly, they classify deleterious (negative) effects on network identity in this way:

- Tying up scarce resources from being used in other relations and/or adaptations detrimental to other relations lead to resource particularity.

- Contingent negative volume effects and/or contingent negative qualitative effect lead to activity irreconcilability.
- Adverse signalling to other relations and/or repulsive connectedness of partners lead to actor-relation incompatibility.

The identity of a company profoundly affects its opportunities to act in the network (Håkansson & Snehota, 1995), for example, in terms of generating the resources and capabilities that are needed. The identity must therefore be cultivated in such a way as to support the aim of the firm in question. This cultivation can, according to Håkansson and Johanson (1988), be undertaken through the operations of the firm and through inter-firm relations and industrial activities. The strategic challenge is then to participate in the process of network evolution in such a way as to become a winner in the sense of becoming a viable partner in the restructured networks that evolve (Wilkinson & Young, 2002).

Methodology

This study uses data collected in the project Healthy Growth of successful mid-scale chains, that is, chains that had managed to combine growth and quality. In Norway, it was not possible to find many successful organic chains because the organic market is less developed, constituting only 1.45% of retail turnover in 2014 (Riksrevisjonen, 2016). The supply chain of Røros Dairy is one of the most successful organic chains in Norway and hence satisfied the requirements for the study.

The problem formulated in the Healthy Growth project required in-depth case-study analysis (Yin, 1994). There is little knowledge about growth in mid-scale organic chains, and there is a need to understand complex relationships, and to understand networks and how they developed during growth processes (Kvam & Bjørkhaug, 2014).

The data collected for the Røros Dairy case study consist mainly of personal interviews and a variety of written materials. A common guide for interviews was developed in the Healthy Growth project. For the Røros Dairy case study, semi-structured interviews were conducted between March and September 2014 and one interview in June 2015 with employees and the manager of Røros Dairy and actors in the dairy network. The data consist of two interviews with the general manager of Røros Dairy and five additional interviews with other actors in the supply chain: (1) two organic farmers and owners representing the cooperative Økomat Røros; (2) the chairman of Røros Food, which is a regional member organization for all local food producers in the Røros region; (3) a representative of Coop, one of three retail chains in Norway and (4) an important representative of Røros Hotel – which has a close relationship with the dairy. We also interviewed a former manager of Røros Dairy, a former board chairperson, and Innovation Norway's[2] regional representative.

To answer the research questions, we asked informants about important actors in the dairy's network for growth, the relationships between actors in the network, and main challenges and discussions connected to growth. Interviews were carried out face to face and then transcribed. A case report was developed that was read and commented on by the main informants (Kvam & Bjørkhaug, 2015). In addition, data were retrieved from the Internet (homepage, Twitter and Facebook) and newspaper articles.

Røros Dairy – and important actors for development and growth

Røros Dairy is located in Røros, a town in the mountain region of south-eastern Norway. Røros was a mining town over the past roughly 400 years and the town and its environs have been placed on UNESCO's World Heritage List. Besides traditional economic activities such as agriculture and forestry, tourism and local food production are important activities for the town and the district.

Local food from Røros is well known in Norway, and Røros Dairy is one of the most important producers. The dairy has been a spearhead for the development of local food in the region, and the close connection with local tourism firms has placed Røros and the surrounding mountainous region on the map as a food region. Røros Dairy is the only organic dairy in Norway. It was established in 2001 as a private limited company. The founders were organic milk producers organized as a cooperative named Økomat Røros, Tine Norwegian Dairies (the big milk cooperative in Norway), Røros municipality and Innovation Norway. The organic farmers were the driving force for its establishment, and their goal was to process all organic milk in the region. Innovation Norway had just established a new 10-year plan to support local food development in 2001, and the initiative at Røros fit very well into this programme. Their financial contribution was decisive for the establishment of the organic initiative.

The milk cooperative, Tine, which represents nearly all milk farmers in Norway, was important in the development of Røros Dairy. Tine, which was the former owner of the dairy at Røros, decided to close it to reduce cost, but different stakeholders with local organic producers wanted to convert the facility into an organic dairy for the region.

Røros Dairy took over machines and equipment from Tine and employed four former Tine employees when Tine closed down. The new dairy produced the traditional products already developed at Røros, such as 'tjukkmelk' (thick sour milk), 'skjørost' (similar to cottage cheese) and 'songraut' (porridge). In addition, the agreement with Tine was that they were free to produce other old and new local dairy specialties (Amilien & Hegnes, 2004) as well as organic light skimmed milk on licence from Tine. The by-product from Tine's licence production was cream that was an important product for Røros Dairy's production of specialized products, such as butter and sour cream.

Organic farmers in the Røros region were members and owners of the cooperative Tine which they wanted to continue even though they had established Røros Dairy. They wanted to continue because membership meant safety for delivering milk and for milk quality. Tine collects the organic milk and pays organic farmers for delivered milk. Røros Dairy then buys the regional organic milk from Tine Råvare, a separate unit in Tine that is responsible for milk collection and sale to actors needing milk. Tine's responsibility is due to the fact that Tine fulfils a market regulator role on behalf of the Norwegian government, which means that it is responsible for regulating the milk market in Norway to secure stable prices for consumers and producers. In 2014, about 35–40 organic milk producers in the region delivered approximately 3.5 million litres of organic milk to Røros Dairy via Tine's system of milk collection and transport. Additionally, the dairy receives about two million litres of organic milk from nearby regions via Tine since 2013 because of lack of sufficient volumes of regional organic milk. The organic farmers organized in the cooperative Økomat Røros are also shareholders of Røros Dairy and are represented in board meetings.

Røros Dairy was challenged when Tine's sale of organic skimmed milk decreased. This decrease resulted in lower amounts of cream from Tine's licence production and a lower volume of production from Røros Dairy. This development was not in accordance with their growth strategy. Therefore, cooperation with Coop was a good opportunity for the dairy and in 2010, Røros Dairy stopped licensing production from Tine and started to produce organic skimmed milk for Coop instead.

Røros Dairy is certified as an organic dairy that differentiates its product from mainstream organic products by emphasizing values/attributes such as local and pure ingredients; traditional products based on rich culinary traditions and handicraft production methods that make the taste unique. Røros Dairy has been active in the qualification of products for the two brands, Protected Geographic Indication (PGI) and Spesialitet [Specialty], and has established a close relationship with Matmerk, a foundation that is responsible for qualifying products for PGI and Specialty (http://www.Matmerk.no). Qualifying products for those two brands has resulted in a lot of positive media attention for the dairy.

During its first years, Røros Dairy sold its products directly to regional customers. In 2005, however, Coop became the first retail chain to sell Røros Dairy's products nationally. Today, the dairy has many customers throughout Norway. These customers can be divided into three groups: the three retail chains in Norway as well as sales to the HoReCa (hotel, restaurant and catering) market, and sales to specialty shops and farm shops nationwide.

Røros Dairy has a closer connection with some customers than with others. An important sales and marketing actor for the dairy in recent years has been Røros Food, a regional actor owned by local food companies, including the Røros Dairy. Røros Food distributes regional products to its members nationwide and supports them in different ways. Another very important relationship is the one with Røros Hotel. In particular, the hotel's director has given ideas, advice and feedback regarding product development and is very aggressive in marketing local products to Røros Hotel's guests. The relationship between Røros Dairy and its local customers is a trust-based relationship in which actors have common values and support each other in different ways.

Røros Dairy has grown from four employees in 2001 to 21 employees in 2014, while sales have increased from 3 million NOK (0.35 million EUR) to 71.5 million NOK (8.1 million EUR). The company has been profitable since 2010 and profitability is growing. Figure 2 shows the development in turnover and results before tax from 2001 to 2014.

The goal in 2014 remains to increase growth given its importance in maintaining the volume of organic milk production in Norway. Increasing the value, and thus the prices of the products, and developing new, distinctive products are important goals for the dairy (Personal interview with the general manager (GM) of Røros Dairy, 2014).

Below, we describe in more detail the relationship between Røros Dairy and the retail chain Coop and the effects of that relationship on both parties. We emphasize the cooperation in licensed production since 2010 that was followed by a huge growth in turnover and gradual profitability for the dairy.

The relationship between Røros Dairy and Coop

Coop has had a connection with Røros Dairy since the latter's establishment. The retailer has been a member of Røros Dairy's board since that time. The agreement with Coop on licensed production in 2010 contributed substantially to growth as shown in Figure 2.

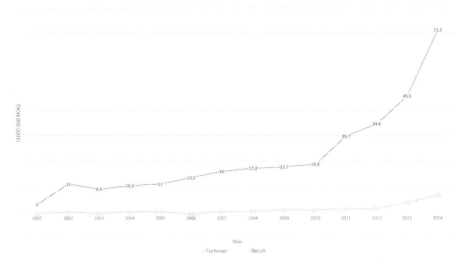

Figure 2. Røros Dairy – growth in turnover and pre-tax results.

Coop was committed to maintaining its position in the organic market with its organic brand, Änglamark. For the retailer, Røros Dairy was the only possible actor left when Tine declined to cooperate with Coop on licensed production. The dairy was still a small actor in the organic milk market in 2009–2010, but Coop knew the company very well. As Coop's representative on the board stated, 'Røros Dairy has a good reputation, and good products that are difficult to copy ... Thus, the products are good for differentiation and sale' (Personal interview with the representative for Coop in the board of Røros Dairy, 2014).

For the dairy, the collaboration with Coop was a conscious choice. According to the general manager, 'it is positive that Coop is a cooperative ... it was the first retail chain that took in products from the dairy ... and we [Coop and Røros Dairy] are based on common values' (i.e. to increase organic production and consumption in Norway) (GM, 2014).

There were some controversies about the agreement with Coop. The main worry was that this cooperation would dilute the dairy's own brand and force its development in a more conventional direction. Organic farmers in the region were generally reluctant to grow. Røros Hotel was afraid that an agreement with Coop would change its focus away from developing its own unique products (Personal interview with the director of Røros Hotel, 2014). Innovation Norway's local representative had to convince headquarters that cooperation with Coop was important for the development and growth of the dairy and that Innovation Norway had to support this cooperation financially. When Røros Dairy's board decided to cooperate with Coop instead of Tine, the main reason was that the dairy needed to grow to increase its profitability (personal interview, Board chairperson of Røros Dairy, 2014). The fact that Coop was similarly organized along cooperative lines just made the decision easier.

The GM of Røros Dairy perceived the relationship with Coop as a good one, citing the fact that Coop had never before cobranded a licensed product. The GM also mentioned that Coop accepted the price that Røros Dairy demanded for the licensed production, which has not always been the case for such products (NOU, 2011). The GM hypothesized that this acceptance is because the dairy is still a small actor in the market.

Producing skimmed milk for Coop results in a cream surplus, which makes it possible to produce more of the existing regional products. Additionally, this cooperation has made it possible to develop a range of new products such as cream and different types of consumer milk. In 2014, about 50% of Røros Dairy's total production was licensed to Coop. The dairy is very conscious that this is an undesirable situation and in the future, they want to be less dependent on Coop and to focus on developing their own unique products (GM, 2014). Coop, on the other hand, is very satisfied with the sale of organic milk and wants to increase cooperation.

Analysing the focal relationship and connected relationships

In this part, we begin by analysing the primary function of the focal relationships (Anderson et al., 1994) between Røros Dairy and Coop.

The primary effects of the focal relationship between Røros Dairy and Coop

The primary function of a focal relationship implies that the interaction of the two partner firms in a focal dyadic relationship will have positive and negative effects on the firms (Anderson et al., 1994). A positive effect of the relationship for both parties is the complementarity of resources. Røros Dairy needed more cream to produce its own established products and new products, and increased demand for light skimmed milk from Coop fortunately gave the dairy an increased amount of cream as a by-product. Increased volume of cream made it possible to produce more own branded products that increased turnover and critically, profitability. The relationship was important for Coop because it gave them the opportunity to offer organic light skimmed milk to their customers. It was additionally very positive to offer organic milk from a well-known local producer with a good reputation in the market.

Another positive effect of the relationship is the cobranding initiated by Coop. Using Røros Dairy's logo and a drawing of the Røros area on the milk carton is good marketing for both actors. This marketing strengthens the local presence and identity of the product. A negative effect expressed by Røros Dairy is its dependency on Coop. The aim over time is to produce only its own branded products. On the other hand, Coop is also dependent on Røros Dairy for the licensed production because the dairy is the only actor interested and willing to produce for them at the moment.

While the primary function of the relationship has both positive and negative effects for Røros Dairy, it is mainly perceived as positive for Coop, which has managed to take advantage of Røros Dairy's position in the organic market by cobranding.

Secondary or network effects of the focal relationship between Røros Dairy and Coop

Using Ritter's (2000) cases of interconnectedness, we are now going to analyse how the focal relationship has affected and is affected by connected relationships, and will thus answer research question 1 (Figure 3).

The connected relationship between Røros Dairy and Tine

The agreement with Coop in 2010 on licensed production meant a termination of the cooperation between Røros Dairy and Tine on the same production. Røros Dairy had established cooperation with a competitor, and Tine had to process organic milk themselves or find another processor if they wished to continue supplying this market. Here, the focal relationship is hindering licensed production in the connected relationship because Røros Dairy could not produce for both parties simultaneously. The connected relationships are decisive for the focal relationship because Tine is the supplier of organic milk to Røros Dairy. A positive effect and a negative effect exist on the focal relationship at the same time, which Ritter (2000) calls 'lack effects'. In this case, Tine is obliged to sell to Røros Dairy; thus, Røros Dairy did not take any risk in changing its licensed production partner.

The focal relationship has also had positive effects on the connected relationship. Because Tine sold only 40% of the organic milk produced in Norway to a premium price, they lost money on this production. The increased sale of organic milk from Coop meant a greater supply of organic milk from Tine to Røros Dairy; Tine received a premium price for a bigger portion of their organic milk production. This is a 'two-way positive effect' or a 'synergy effect' where the relationships support each other (Ritter, 2000).

The focal relationship has made Røros Dairy more independent of Tine and free to produce whatever products it wanted although it was in competition with Tine's products. This situation has had a negative effect on the connected relationship to Tine because they

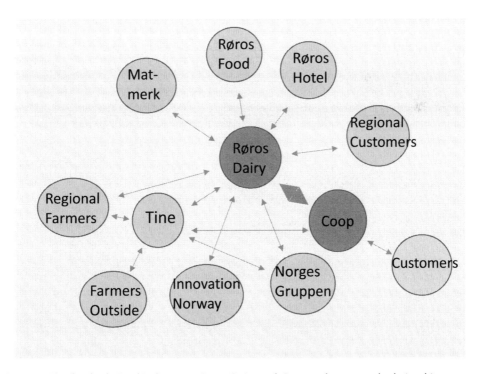

Figure 3. The focal relationship between Røros Dairy and Coop and connected relationships.

became competitors. This case is also categorized as a 'lack effect' (Ritter, 2000), that is, a situation in which a positive impact and a negative impact coexist.

On the other hand, increased demand for organic milk is a positive development also for Tine because it is the only supplier and controls this resource. Thus, the focal relationship may have a positive influence on the relationship between Røros Dairy and Tine over time.

The connected relationship between Røros Dairy and organic farmers

The decreased sale of organic milk from Tine reduced the volume of organic milk sold as well as the price Tine paid to organic farmers. The focal relationship implied increased demand for organic milk. Since 2013, Røros Dairy has had to process organic milk from farmers in nearby regions to satisfy demand. The focal relationship influenced the connected relationship between Røros Dairy and regional farmers in a positive way because they reached the goal to process all organic milk in the region. Some regional farmers were sceptical about the cooperation with Coop initially and about the dairy's growth ambitions. On the other hand, if demand for organic milk increased further, they expected that the price for organic milk would increase. We recognize a 'two-way positive effect' or 'synergy effects' where the focal relationship has influenced the connected relationships in a positive way because of the increased sale of organic milk (Ritter, 2000).

The connected relationship between Røros Dairy and Norgesgruppen

Cooperation with Coop made it impossible, because of the lack of capacity, for Røros Dairy to cooperate with the other two retail chains in the short run. The interconnectedness between the focal relationship and the connected one meant that the retail chain NorgesGruppen was excluded from cooperation on licensed production. Thus, the focal relationship had a hindrance effect on the connected relationship (Ritter, 2000). On the other hand, the focal relationship leads to increased production of Røros Dairy's own and new branded products and all customers of Røros Dairy have benefited from a larger volume and new products. This is a typical 'two-way positive effect' or 'synergy effect' (Ritter, 2000).

The connected relationships between Røros Dairy and local customers

The director of Røros Hotel was one of the actors who was very sceptical about the focal relationship and was afraid it would damage the dairy's brand and identity. That the focal relationship provided the dairy with more resources and greater capacity to focus on product development was important to its relationship with Røros Hotel. This was also the situation for the local HoReCa market in general. In such connected customer relationships, there were no reverse effects, that is, the connected relationships did not affect the focal relationship. Ritter (2000) called this an 'assistance effect'. The focal relationship has increased the volume distributed by Røros Food on behalf of the dairy. This increase has been important for the increased turnover and profitability of Røros Food. The effect is also a one-sided positive effect, as above, with no reverse effect on the focal relationship. Instead, it has an 'assistance effect' (Ritter, 2000).

Connected relationship between Røros Dairy and Matmerk
The focal relationship indirectly influenced product development and thus the connected relationship between Røros Dairy and Matmerk. The focal relationship resulted in increased turnover and profitability, and made it possible to focus even more on product development and to qualify traditional and quality products for Matmerk's labels. This is a positive domino effect from the focal relationship to connected relationships (Hertz, 1998 as cited by Ritter, 2000). Positive reviews of Røros Dairy and its products may affect the focal relationship in a good way by creating customer interest in licensed products. There is a 'two-way positive effect' of the interconnected relationship, or synergy effects, according to Ritter (2000).

Connected relationship between Røros Dairy and Innovation Norway
Innovation Norway's[3] (IN) head office was very skeptical about RD's cooperation with Coop and was concerned that this cooperation would dilute the brand. Following lengthy consideration and discussion, IN did support Røros Dairy in developing its relationship with Coop – a support that was crucial for establishing the focal relationship between Røros Dairy and Coop. The focal relationship has supported the growth of the dairy, which is an important goal for both the dairy and for IN's support schemes for local food firms. Thus, there is a 'two-way positive effect' (Ritter, 2000).

According to our first research question, about how relationships influence each other, we clearly see that actors in the network context of the focal firm are interconnected in myriad ways. Results also show that there are different effects, both positive and negative, and different categories of effects; these results are in accordance with Ritter's (2000) findings.

Positive and negative effects on network identity

In this part, we answer our second research question, how the focal relationship between Røros Dairy and Coop influences the focal firm's network identity. Has the focal firm managed to maintain its identity as an organic quality-oriented producer despite cooperation with the conventional actor, Coop?

The main resource in our study, organic milk, depends on resources being transferred from connected relationships on the supply side, that is, from Tine and organic farmers. Product developed in the focal relationship led to increased demand for resources from these connected relationships, and the focal relationship had positive synergy effects on resource use of connected suppliers. According to Anderson et al. (1994), this synergy effects have positive effects on the focal firm's network identity.

Cream, the by-product from the licensed production, and the availability of organic milk from nearby regions made it possible for Røros Dairy to combine these resources with resources from other relationships and to transfer/sell to customers in connected relationships. Transferability of resources in connected relationships has positive effects on connected actors in the network and thus on the focal firm's network identity (Anderson et al., 1994).

Anderson et al. (1994) suggest anticipated activity complementarity where the connected relationships are contingent on activities performed in the focal relationship. The situation in our case is that connected relationships in the focal firm's supply chain are contingent on the licensed production to increase supply of organic milk from the supplier side. Dairy customers are also dependent on the increased production of organic milk in the focal relationship because increased production gives the dairy resources to increase volume on existing products and to develop new organic products in cooperation with Røros Hotel or others. Thus, activities performed in the focal relationship affect positively activities in connected relationships along the supply chain. Activities influencing Tine and organic farmers are typically volume based. The activities connected to customers are both volume and quality based. These activities seem to strengthen the focal firm's network identity (Anderson et al., 1994).

The relationship between Coop and Røros Dairy signals that the dairy is a serious actor in the organic network in Norway. It shows that the dairy is no longer only a small processor, but a significant actor to consider. The dairy will be viewed as being stronger in resource terms when it can deliver substantial resources to its connected partner, Coop. Requests from the two competing retail chains about cooperation confirm the perception that Røros Dairy is an attractive partner for cooperation. Nevertheless, cobranding with Coop shows that they value Røros Dairy as an organic quality-oriented producer and not only as an organic mainstream actor. Without cobranding, the stream of resources in this licensed production would not have affected Røros Dairy's identity. Although Tine has experienced both negative and positive effects of the focal relationship, the focal relationship has made Røros Dairy even more attractive as a partner for Tine. Hence, a negative effect of the focal relationships may not imply a negative perception of the focal firm's identity.

The ongoing activity focusing on developing new, unique products from Røros Dairy signals that it is a local actor intent on creating alternative products. Cooperation with local actors such as Røros Hotel confirms this perception and confirms the qualification of products in cooperation with Matmerk. Attention from the media strengthens this signal and the perception of Røros Dairy's identity as a substantial and active actor in the organic-quality food market. The focal firm has not experienced any negative effect from the focal relationships on the customer's side. To the contrary, the dairy is still a very attractive partner for organic-quality food customers. The fact that IN still supports the dairy financially shows that they also perceive the dairy as an organic quality-oriented producer.

There are no negative effects on network identity. Some network actors were afraid that the focal relationship and cooperation on licensed production would take the focus away from other activities supporting the identity the dairy want to convey. Activities undertaken by the focal firm have strengthened its identity as an attractive partner for both larger companies and smaller actors in the organic foods network.

The fact that Røros Dairy had a favourable position in the network when the relationship with Coop was established was important for maintaining the dairy's identity. Also, the fact that the actors in the focal relationship had much the same values and goals concerning organic production and sale seems to be important (Dyer & Nobeoka, 2000). In addition, Røros Dairy's ongoing focus on product development in cooperation with local and other partners seems to be important for maintaining its identity as a regional organic-quality producer. The close connection with the local food network at Røros most probably does play an important role in the dairy's network identity, as being part of a network that posits a strong connection between identity and practice (Wenger, 1998).

Discussion and conclusion

While previous literature has suggested that growth in organic values-based chains and relations with conventional actors may imply conventionalization of the organic chains (Guthman, 2004; Mount, 2012; Noe & Alrøe, 2011), our study indicates that such collaboration may function without the quality-oriented actor losing its main values. Using the IMP perspective has made possible a better and more complex understanding of the interconnectedness of actors in a network and how they may influence each other and respective network identities.

Regarding effects of connected relationships, our findings show a more complex picture than do Ritter's (2000) findings concerning cases he defined. When we try to capture the development aspects of a firm as part of its network, analysis clearly shows that the network effects may change over time. This changes over time is in accordance with the IMP theory where a network is supposed to be under constant evolution that necessarily implies changes in relationships (Håkansson & Snehota, 1995). Furthermore, when a relationship is established, there are expectations of future effects that are not clear and/or are not fulfilled from the start of the relationship. Future expectations are difficult to relate to, but may be very important for the decision to cooperate and therefore should be included in the analysis in one way or the other.

Another dimension that is lacking is that two actors may cooperate in different areas simultaneously, which also is emphasized in La Rocca (2013). When one activity stops, another activity may benefit from the negative effect on the first. This was observed in the connected relationship between Røros Dairy and Tine, when the partner for licensed production changed. Thus, relationships may influence each other in both positive and negative ways simultaneously and according to Anderson et al. (1994), different relationships can affect each other in the actor, activity, and/or resource dimensions simultaneously.

Concerning the concept 'network identity' and the framework for analysis according to Anderson et al. (1994), both have proved valuable for understanding the effects of relationships on network identity. However, there is room for further elaboration on the identity concept within the IMP tradition. According to Anderson et al. (1994), the concept 'network identity' captures the perceived attractiveness or repulsiveness of a firm as an exchange partner. Attractiveness does not necessarily imply connectedness to the identity that the firm wants to convey. For Røros Dairy, Coop was interesting as a partner mainly because Røros Dairy needed to increase the volume of cream. Thus, it was important for the dairy also to be attractive as a volume producer. Hence, it might have been important to establish and develop different identities to maintain the one the firm wanted to convey most.

How can the IMP perspective contribute to our understanding of organic chains and how they develop? The IMP perspective considers firms as embedded in a broader network where the actions of a single firm are confronted with the actions of other firms with partly overlapping and partly opposite goals (Håkansson & Ford, 2002). Thus, one important aim must be to become a preferable partner in the network. Røros Dairy's identity was built in close cooperation with regional actors and other actors in the supply chain by emphasizing organic and regional qualities. Furthermore, the dairy collaborated with external partners, such as Matmerk and Innovation Norway, that contributed to strengthening its identity. The path to become an attractive partner seems to be to cooperate with partners that (partly) share your values and thus, each strengthens the other.

Using the IMP perspective on a successful and unique case has implications for the way it can be useful for managers of organic values-based firms. Although settings and firms will differ, and although it is not possible to predict the direction of development of a network or to forecast final effects of any network action (Håkansson & Ford, 2002), it is possible to learn from how a successful firm has developed in its network. The case study gives insight into how different actors in a firm's network, both chain actors and other actors, together play an important role for development and growth. Furthermore, the case can be valuable in showing how the focal firm has managed to maintain its network identity in the cooperation with a large retail chain. The knowledge can prove useful for business managers on the importance of understanding and consciously interacting in both new and established relations in ways that may improve the firm's position in the network and its possibility to strengthen its network identity and hence affect its opportunities. This is particularly important in the quality food market where a change in network identity from a quality actor to a mainstream organic actor may have a decisive effect on profitability and survival.

Generally, this case shows aspects of the transition of the Norwegian food system since early 2000. Conventional actors are not so 'conventional' anymore, and they have adapted sustainability values – but to varying degrees. Nevertheless, there are still challenges for organic quality-oriented firms in scaling up, and only a very few organic chains in Norway have managed to grow (Kvam & Bjørkhaug, 2013).

A challenge in the Norwegian organic foods market is that customers are not willing to pay a much higher price for organic than for conventional products. One important reason for this is that the extra values of organic products are not communicated to customers. Røros Dairy is very aware of this communications failure and emphasizes a variety of communication channels towards consumers, for example, use of labels and demos in shops. For smaller actors in the market with fewer resources, such activities are too resource-demanding (Kvam, Magnus, & Stræte, 2014).

Røros Dairy managed to adapt values when scaling up without damaging their identity, but this is not always the situation (Mount, 2012). In Norway, few alternative food chains exist and it is still not necessarily easy to find a partner that supports the values one's firm wants to convey. Besides licensed production of organic products for retail chains, another development trait in Norway is that retail chains focus on vertical integration of organic- and quality-oriented actors. Then, the organic firm's destiny is laid in the hands of the big actor, and the fear is that the organic firm's original qualities and values will be lost.

An interesting avenue for further research would be to develop the dynamic aspects further, as part of Ritter's (2000) categories on the effects of relationships. Furthermore, it would be interesting to elaborate on the concept of 'network identity' and its different aspects, such as the focal firm's perception of and development of its own identity, as well as other network actors' perceptions of the focal firm's identity.

Notes

1. Healthy Growth is a Core Organic II project financed by The Research Council of Norway.

2. Innovation Norway is a national public support institution for small and medium-sized firms (www.innovasjonorge.no).
3. Innovation Norway is a national public support body directed towards supporting small- and medium-sized firms (www.innovasjonorge.no).

Disclosure statement

No potential conflict of interest was reported by the authors.

Funding

This work was supported by The Research Council of Norway [grant number 227789].

References

Amilien, V., & Hegnes, A. W. (2004). The cultural smell of fermented fish, about the development of a local product in Norway. *Journal of Food, Agriculture and Environment (JFAE), 2*(1), 141–147.
Anderson, J. C., Håkansson, H., & Johanson, J. (1994). Dyadic business relationships within a business network context. *Journal of Marketing, 58*(October), 1–15. doi:10.2307/1251912
Axelsson, B., & Easton, G. (1992). *Industrial networks – A new view of reality*. London: Routledge.
Barney, J. (1991). Firms resources and sustained competitive advantage. *Journal of Management, 17*(1), 99–120.
Cook, C., & Emerson, R. (1978). Power, equity and commitment in exchange networks. *American Sociological Review, 43*, 721–739. doi:10.2307/2094546
Dyer, J. H., & Nobeoka, K. (2000). Creating and managing a high-performance knowledge-sharing network: The Toyota case. *Strategic Management Journal, 21*, 234–367. doi:10.1002/(SICI)1097-0266 (200003)21:3<345:AID-SMJ96>3.0.Co;2-N
Emerson, R. (1972). Exchange theory, Part I: Exchange relations and network structures. In M. Zelditch & B. Anderson (Eds.), *Sociological theories in progress* (Vol. 2, pp. 58–87). Boston, MA: Houghton Mifflin.
Ford, D., Gadde, L.-E., Håkansson, H., Lundgren, A., Snehota, I., Turnbull, P., & Wilson, D. (1998). *Managing business relationships*. London: Wiley.
Ford, D., Gadde, L.-E., Håkansson, H., & Snehota, I. (2003). *Managing business relationships* (3rd ed.). Chichester: John Wiley.
Guthman, J. (2004). The trouble with 'organic lite' in California: A rejoinder to the 'conventionalisation' debate. *Sociologia Ruralis, 44*(3), 301–316. doi:10.1111/j.1467-9523.2004.00277.x
Håkansson, H., & Ford, D. (2002). How should companies interact in business networks? *Journal of Business Research, 55*, 133–139. doi:10.1016/S0148-2963(00)00148-X
Håkansson, H., Ford, D., Gadde, L.-E., Snehota, I., & Waluszewski, A. (2009). *Business in networks*. Chichester: John Wiley.
Håkansson, H., & Johanson, J. (1988). Formal and informal cooperation strategies in international industrial networks. In: F. J. Contractor & P. Lorange (Eds.), *International business* (pp. 369–379). Lexington, MA: Lexington Books.
Håkansson, H., & Snehota, I. (Eds.). (1995). *Developing relationships in business networks*. London: Routledge.
Hertz, S. (1998). Domino effects in international networks. *Journal of Business-to-Business Marketing, 5*(3), 3–31. doi:10.1300/J033v05n03_02
Holmen, E., & Pedersen, A.-C. (2003). Strategizing through analyzing and influencing the network horizon. *Industrial Marketing Management, 32*, 409–418. doi:10.1016/S0019-8501(03)00014-2

Ilbery, B., Courtney, P., Kirwan, J., & Maye, D. (2010). Marketing concentration and geographical dispersion: A survey of organic farms in England and Wales. *British Food Journal*, *112*(9), 962–975. doi:10.1108/00070701011074345

Knutsen, M. T., Halberg, N., Olesen, J. E., Byrne, J., Iyver, V., & Toly, N. (2006). Global trends in agriculture and food systems. In N. Halberg, H. F. Alrøe, M. T. Knudsen, & E. S. Kristensen (Eds.), *Global development of organic agriculture – challenges and prospects* (pp. 1–48). Wallingford: CABI.

Kvam, G. T., & Bjørkhaug, H. (2013). *Volume growth in quality food firms – Lessons and reflections from Norway*. Retrieved from http://www.florenceesrs2013.com/wp-content/uploads/2012/07/ESRS2013_eProceedings.pdf

Kvam, G. T., & Bjørkhaug, H. (2014). *State of the art review – On healthy growth initiatives in the mid-scale values-based chain of organic food*. Report as part of the Healthy Growth project. Retrieved from http://orgprints.org/25620/7/25520.pdf

Kvam, G. T., & Bjørkhaug, H. (2015). *Full case study report: Røros Dairy, Norway*. Centre for Rural Research, Trondheim. Retrieved from www://orgprints.org/

Kvam, G. T., & Magnus, T., Stræte, E. P. (2014, May). Product strategies for growth in niche food firms. *British Food Journal*, Research paper, *116*(4). doi:10.1108/BFJ-06-2011-0168

La Rocca, A. (2013). Approaching inter-actors in the business landscape. *The IMP Journal*, *7*(3), 171–179.

Marsden, T., Banks, J., & Bristow, G. (2000). Food supply chain approach: Exploring their role in rural development. *Sociologia Ruralis*, *40*(4), 424–438. doi:10.1111/1467-9523.00158

Marsden, T., & Smith, E. (2005). Ecological entrepreneurship: Sustainable development in local communities through quality food production and local branding. *Geoforum*, *36*, 440–451. doi:10.1016/j.geoforum.2004.07.008

Miles, R., & Snow, C. C. (1992). Causes of failure of network organizations. *California Management Review*, *32*(4), 53–72. doi:10.2307/41166703

Mount, P. (2012). Growing local food: Scale and local food systems governance. *Agriculture and Human Values*, *29*(1), 107–121. doi:10.1007/s10460-011-9331-0

Noe, E. (2007). *National synthesis report on case studies in Denmark*. Retrieved from http://www.cofami.org/fileadmin/documents-cofami/WP4-nat-synt-DK.pdf

Noe, E., & Alrøe, H. F. (2011). Quality, coherence and cooperation: A framework for studying the mediation of qualities in food networks and collective marketing strategies. *International Journal of the Sociology of Agriculture and Food*, *18*(1), 12–27.

NOU. (2011). Mat, makt og avmakt – om styrkeforholdet i verdikjeden for mat. 2011:4.

Ostrom, M. R., & Jussaume, R. A., Jr. (2007). Assessing the significance of directs farmer-consumer linkages as a change strategy in Washington State: Civic or opportunistic? In C. C. Hinrichs & T. Lyson (Eds.), *Remaking the North American food system* (pp. 235–259). Lincoln: University of Nebraska Press.

Riksrevisjonen. (2016). *Riksrevisjonens undersøking av arbeidet til styresmaktene for å nå måla om økologisk landbruk*. Dokument 3:7 (2015–2016). Oslo: Riksrevisjonen.

Ritter, T. (2000). A framework for analyzing interconnectedness of relationships. *Industrial Marketing Management*, *29*, 317–326. doi:10.1016/S0019-8501(00)00108-5

Schermer, M., Matscher, A., & Borec, A. (2010, July 4–7). *Organization of supply chains for mountain products to meet consumer's expectations – Cases from Slovenia and Austria*. 9th European IFSOA Symposium, Vienna.

Schermer, M., Renting, H., & Ostindie, H. (2011). Collective farmers' marketing initiatives in Europe: Diversity, contextuality and dynamics. *International Journal of the Sociology of Agriculture and Food*, *18*(1), 1–11.

Sonnino, R., & Marsden, T. (2006). Beyond the divide: Rethinking relationships between alternative and conventional food networks in Europe. *Journal of Economic Geography*, *6*(2), 181–199. doi:10.1093/jeg/lbi006

Stevenson, G. W., & Pirog, R. (2008). Values-based supply chains: Strategies for agrifood enterprises of the middle. In T. A. Lyson, G. W. Stevenson, & R. Welsh (Eds.), *Food and the mid-level farm:*

Renewing an agriculture of the middle (pp. 119–143). Cambridge: The MIT Press. Retrieved from http://www.agofthemiddle.org/papers/valuechain.pdf

Stevenson, S. (2009). *Values-based food supply chains: Executive summary* – Country Natural Beef, CROPP/Organic Valley, Shepherds's Grain and Red Tomato. Retrieved from http://www.agofthemiddle.org/pubs/vcexecsum.pdf

Wenger, E. (1998). *Communities of practice: Learning, meaning, and identity.* New York, NY: Cambridge University Press.

Wernerfelt, B. (1984). A resource-based view of the firm. *Strategic Management Journal, 5*(2), 171–180. doi:10.1002/smj.4250050207

Wilkinson, I., & Young, L. (2002). On cooperating: Firms, relations and networks. *Journal of Business Research, 55*, 123–132. doi:10.1016/S0148-2963(00)00147-8

Yamagishi, T., Gillmore, M. R., & Cook, K. S. (1988). Network connections and the distribution of power in exchange networks. *American Journal of Sociology, 93*(4), 833–851. doi:10.1086/228826

Yin, R. (1994). *Case study research, design and methods, applied social research methods series* (Vol. 5). Thousand Oaks, CA: Sage.

It's never too late to join the revolution! – Enabling new modes of production in the contemporary Danish food system

Martin Hvarregaard Thorsøe, Chris Kjeldsen and Egon Noe

ABSTRACT

The Danish food system has undergone a transition in the past 10–20 years, in which new quality conventions have evolved. Examples include increasing organic production and consumption, and increasing interest in local food, experience, community, taste and gastronomy. This article explores what influences if and how these new food trends are expressed in the food system. We conduct a comparative case study involving three product categories: craft beer, specialty flour and organic broilers. Craft beer and specialty flour have undergone a revolution, in which new flavours, products, practices and social relations are generated; by contrast, organic broilers have remained a relatively stable product category. The case studies demonstrate that the revolution is not just taking place in one domain, but it implies a multidimensional reconfiguration of the food system where an emphasis on multiple quality aspects and diversification of the product category is important. However, food trends are not the invention of the individual producer, but serve as common conventions that products can be related to, although their interpretation is not pre-given. In addition, a transition presupposes a shared vision and a coordination of activities among the actors in the food system or the mobilization of new actors who share this vision.

1. Introduction

In the past 10–20 years, the Danish food system has been influenced by several new tendencies, including increasing organic production and consumption, a growing interest in local food production and an emphasis on experience, community, taste and gastronomy. In consequence, various product categories have been revolutionized by the introduction of new tastes, consumer cultures and production practices. Although food trends change, the trends are not always expressed in all product categories, and our ambition with this article is to explore what influences if and how new food trends are expressed in the food system.

In the Danish food market, a number of changes have occurred and this market therefore forms a good base for a case study on the foundations for such changes. In particular, we will explore the expression of new food trends by comparing two cases where the food market has been revolutionized (craft beer and specialty flour) with one case where the market has not evolved to the same extent (organic broilers have a market share of less than 1% where the average organic market share is around 8%).

It is important to understand how food quality evolves; as consumers increasingly request food products with added value and differentiated qualities (Meldgaard et al., 2015), improvements in primary production presuppose the mediation of these qualities in the market (Thorsøe & Noe, 2016). In addition, the production of differentiated food products is an important development pathway for many small-scale food producers (Renting, Marsden, & Banks, 2003; Stræte, 2008; Tregear, Arfini, Belletti, & Marescotti, 2007).

The question is explored in four steps. First, we explore the development which has taken place in the Danish food system in the past 10–15 years, highlighting the emerging food quality trends. Second, we explore the concept of food quality and investigate the various aspects of food quality and its conceptualization within convention theory (CT), and sketch out our analytical strategy. Third, we conduct three case studies: (1) the (re)introduction of flour from old grain varieties, (2) the emergence of a craft beer sector and (3) the production of organic broilers. Four, we compare the three cases and discuss the opportunities and barriers for implementing new food trends in the food system.

2. New quality conventions in the Danish food system

In the following section we explore four notable changes that have taken place in the Danish food system in the past 10–15 years as a background for evaluating how they are expressed in the three case studies.

First, increasing focus on organics. Consumption of organics in Denmark has increased continuously for the past 30 years and today accounts for 8% of the market, which has exceeded the Danish production capacity for several food items, and has been accompanied by a growth in the import of foreign organic products (Thorsøe, 2015). In particular, the demand for organic food is driven by a focus on health and animal welfare (Christensen, Olsen, Kærgård, & Dubgaard, 2014).

Second, there is an increasing focus on food as the material context of new experiences and communities. For instance, in a coordinated yearly event Danish organic dairy producers put their dairy cows out to grass, attracting around 200,000 spectators on 70 different organic farms in just one day (Økodag, 2014). Furthermore, several large food festivals have emerged that attract up to 30,000 visitors over a weekend where they interact with food producers, NGOs and learn about food production and cuisine. Community building around food has also become more important with the establishment of the Food Communities (Fødevarefællesskaberne) in 2008, which are networks of urban consumers sourcing local organic produce, where members are committed to volunteer work (Thorsøe & Kjeldsen, 2016). The Food Communities have quickly become a prominent new feature with more than 5000 members in 28 smaller communities.

Third, there is an increasing focus on local food, and origin has become an important factor in consumers' decisions to purchase particular products, reflecting a growing interest in the geographical origin of foods (Eriksen & Sundbo, 2016). Recently, there has been an increase in the direct sale of meat, dairy, flour and vegetables, for instance, reflected in an increase in the number of farm shops from 1200 in 2007 to 2300 in 2013 (Meldgaard et al., 2015). Furthermore, one of the two large supermarket chains, COOP, has given direct market access to selected producers in their local supermarket.

Fourth, taste and gastronomy have become prominent new tendencies, following the inception of the New Nordic Food Cuisine in 2004, which is based on the virtues of 'taste', as well as local, seasonal and traditional products of the highest quality (The Nordic Council of Ministers, 2012). According to Hermansen (2012), New Nordic Food (NNF) is a way to express identity in the Nordic countries, an 'exercise in nostalgia'. However, NNF is as much a construct as it is a rediscovery of a historically rooted food culture, and the 'tastemakers' in the NNF are a group of chefs and food critics, who have discerned the taste of the Nordic for the general public (Byrkjeflot, Pedersen, & Svejenova, 2013).

It is important to emphasize that there is also a growing divide among Danish consumers, where some consumers have embraced these new trends, but, for example, around half of the population claim to be indifferent to organic production (Lund, Andersen, & O'Doherty Jensen, 2013). The changes which have taken place in the Danish food system are in many ways parallel to the development in other Scandinavian countries and in the northern part of Europe, but Denmark has a more industrialized agricultural production than other Scandinavian countries to begin with (Halkier, 2017; Holm et al., 2012; Kjærnes, Harvey, & Warde, 2007; Kvam & Bjørkhaug, 2013). Southern Europe, on the other hand, has a long tradition for many of these food trends such as local and regional food, terroir, direct food trade, gastronomy and celebration of commodities in food festivals. Compared with, for instance, France and Italy, the expression of the new food trends is still burgeoning in Denmark (Kjeldsen, Kidmose, & Kristensen, 2014). However, Denmark has a much higher share of organic consumption (Willer & Lernoud, 2014).

3. Understanding and analysing food quality

It follows from the developments mentioned above, that new qualities have emerged within the Danish foodscape. In the agro-food literature, this phenomenon has been labelled 'the quality turn' (Goodman, 2003). The quality turn has been explored from various research perspectives, such as possibilities for regional development (Renting et al., 2003), globalization (Raynolds, 2004) and social and environmental justice (Hinrichs & Allen, 2008).

However, Stræte and Marsden (2006) argue for a need to expand the scope of research on quality and food and Moragues-Faus and Sonnino (2012) argue that much of the research is single case studies, concentrating primarily on the agency of the producer networks, thus paying little attention to the wider socioeconomic and territorial context in which the food systems operate. Hence, much attention is given to the market actors without conceptualizing the wider social domain in the accounts of how new food qualities emerge (Tregear, 2011). One of the academic challenges that is still pressing is to understand how these new qualities can be stabilized and sustained and how new constellations of actors and practices within the food market emerge, both across as well as within specific product categories. Another challenge is to avoid shallow utilization of case study results.

In this paper we deploy a theoretical approach based on CT as developed by Salais and Storper (1992) and Boltanski and Thevenot (2006). In CT, conventions have been defined as systems of reciprocal expectations about the behaviour of others (Ponte, 2016; Salais & Storper, 1992; Storper & Salais, 1997), or more specifically 'shared templates for interpreting situations and planning courses of action in mutually comprehensive ways that involve social accountability providing a basis for judging the appropriateness of action by self and others' (Biggart & Beamish, 2003, p. 444). Conventions can thus be used as a heuristic tool to understand how social practice within markets is coordinated. Within CT, conventions are conceived as constituting different 'worlds' within markets. It follows from this that within CT it does not make sense to talk about 'the market' as a singular entity – instead, markets are seen as a multiverse phenomenon.

CT is a well-established approach within the field of agro-food studies, in particular within the sociology of food (Bernzen & Braun, 2014; Coq-Huelva, Sanz-Cañada, & Sánchez-Escobar, 2014; Ponte, 2016), but also within research fields such as geography (Barnett, 2014; Mansfield, 2003) and political economy (Ponte, 2016; Ponte & Gibbon, 2005; Renard, 2005). CT has been applied to understand the emergence and growth of 'alternative' food networks across a range of different food markets in Europe and North America. One of the overall contributions of CT has been to a more pluralistic understanding of how quality shapes production, exchange and consumption on food markets as conventions are seen as an organizing element of actors in the food system. In a recent review, Ponte (2016) emphasizes that the implications of CT have been far-reaching in relation to the discussion of quality and how quality shapes organization, coordination and exchange. Some of the specific implications of CT include (1) that there is no generally accepted understanding of quality, (2) that quality is evaluated through social interaction in different ways relative to which convention is used to justify action, (3) there is a direct link between understandings of quality and the social organization of production and exchange, (4) different degrees of ease in translating conventions in the food system can be an important factor in shaping their governance and (5) that the same agro-food companies may draw on different quality conventions, or combinations of these (Ponte, 2016, p. 20).

The transition of food qualities is a complex process that implies the coordination of various activities in the entire food system, including primary production, processing, retail and consumption (Carolan, 2011; Stræte, 2008). Hence, food quality cannot be reduced to a physical attribute of individual food products, nor can it be reduced to an attribute of the social organization evolving around food. Food qualities are intricately linked with values and the CT framework emphasizes the process whereby food items attain value as a property of its relations with other actors in the food system (Stark, 2011). In this way we derive explanations that are specific to each product category, but may draw on similar ideas concerning what is valuable. However, the development of food qualities cannot be reduced to a one-dimensional process, but a range of factors must be taken into account, including consumption, culture, knowledge, technology, discourses, materiality and market organization (Geels, 2004).

Analytically we explore how different conventions are applied in the organization of the food system and how the different actors relate to these conventions. We will focus on the four food trends: increasing organic consumption, growing interest in local food production, experience and community building, and taste and gastronomy. In this article we will unfold how they function as conventions that are translated and embedded into the different product categories.

4. Methods

The three cases are very different, not only in terms of product materiality, but also the development that has taken place within the product categories. In response, the cases are described using a standardized procedure. Initially we produced a timeline of the development in the three different product categories, drawing on three different sources of empirical data. The market development was characterized using statistical data acquired via the Danish Statistical Survey and various commodity-specific databases. Secondly, we explored the media coverage of the product categories in five different media (Politiken, Jyllands-Posten, Information, Økologi og Erhverv, Økologisk) extracted from the Infomedia database (records dating from January 2000 until December 2015). We used a combination of different keywords, relevant for each product category, to capture all relevant articles, but primarily focused on articles longer than 1000 words. This data collection produced around 100 documents, which were read to identify important events, providing a background for understanding the development and a basis for the interview guide.

Subsequently, we conducted 10 in-depth, semi-structured interviews with key stakeholders lasting an hour or more in the fall of 2015 and spring of 2016 (three grain producers, five organic broiler producers and processors, two brewers) (Brinkmann & Kvale, 2008). All respondents were selected because they have been prominent actors in the food system for a number of years and have specific insights into the development in the product categories. In addition, we conducted a workshop with producers and processors of organic broilers, which has been used as input data (Thorsøe, Laursen, & Noe, 2015). Interview guides all addressed the following five themes: (1) development history (company and product category), (2) business strategies, (3) collaborations and relationships, (4) innovation in the food system and (5) opportunities and barriers for implementing new quality conventions. The interviews and the focus group were recorded and subsequently transcribed verbatim. Transcriptions were then open-coded (Corbin, 1998). Quotes were selected to highlight the recurring themes and subsequently translated into English.

Following the description of the three cases we employed a mode of analysis that included within-case methods like process tracing in combination with a qualitative cross-case comparison (George & Bennett, 2005). Methodologically, a case study is well suited to analysing complex social phenomena such as the development of food qualities (Flyvbjerg, 2006). Furthermore, it enables an in-debt inquiry, allowing us to include various data sources in the analysis. Our ambition therefore is not alone to explain the behaviour of the actors, but also the context and the development over time, such that the behaviour of the actors becomes meaningful to outsiders.

5. Case study results

The following section will present the results of the three case studies.

5.1. Specialty flour

Around year 2000, flour was a relatively uniform product category and the selection was restricted to a few wheat and rye flour products. Quality differentiation was restricted to wholemeal or plain and specialty flour was a niche product for a narrow consumer segment, only retailed in health food stores. Today there is a great diversity in the product category and an average supermarket offers a selection of flour from several different grain varieties, brands, grinding techniques and both organic and conventional versions.

The change is observable several places in the food system. Farmers have begun to cultivate old grain varieties, and the eight most dominant old grain varieties now cover an estimated 2500 ha (roughly corresponding to 8000 t and a wholesale value of €30 million) (ØL, 2015). However, statistics describing the development are very sparse and unreliable, as the varieties are not formally registered in the EU common catalogue of varieties of agricultural plant species. The introduction of specialty flour has almost tripled the average household spending on organic flour in the period 2006–2014 and organic flour is one of the most popular organic commodities with a 23% market share (DST, 2015). A number of new mills have now started a dedicated production of specialty flour.

The development was driven by engaged organic farmers, who were discontented with the selection of grain varieties on offer. According to one of the key Danish figures in organic plant breeding, 'the quality of our bread has simply been shameful for a number of years [...] poor bread begins with the grains in the field and that triggered my engagement with plant breeding'. In organic production the use of pesticides is prohibited, and the use of fertilizer is restricted, but these concerns are not taken into consideration by conventional seed producers, making the conventional seeds unsuitable for organic production. In addition, conventional wheat has been bred with a particular emphasis on industrial utilization, favouring proteins that form long glutinous strings rather than short strings that are more suitable for home-baking. These issues motivated a group of organic producers to search for alternatives within the holdings of the Nordic Genetic Resource Center (NorGen). During the 1990s, Danish famers, along with colleagues from other countries in Scandinavia, experimented with various varieties of wheat, rye and oats, selecting and multiplying seeds.

Since the beginning of the 1990s the small-scale mill and bakery Aurion has sold spelt flour in farm shops and health food stores. However, specialty flour remained unknown to the general public until the NNF movement caught on and celebrity chefs started to endorse and include them in their dishes. This new alliance brought old grain varieties out of the health food stores and into gourmet restaurants, specialty food stores and eventually onto supermarket shelves. Growers experimented with many different grain varieties and they selected one particularly popular variety of wheat, 'Ølandshvede' (originating form Öland, Sweden), as the vanguard variety and today around two-thirds of sales of old grain varieties are attributed to this variety. According to another key figure of organic plant breeding, marketing 'Ølandshvede' was a deliberate and coordinated attempt to highlight some of the obstacles facing organic plant breeders:

> we had the feeling that we would encounter a legal obstacle, so we made an agreement with the Danish AgriFish Agency, that they would look the other way until there was a new common catalogue [...], and we have deliberately taken advantage of that, by making 'ølandshvede' so big that they cannot shut us down now even if they wanted to.

The diversification of the flour market has been a bottom-up process and it has caught on outside conventional sales channels. It involves a number of changes for producers, processers and consumers, illustrating a complex transition throughout the entire food system. Farmers need to manage their own stock of seeds, as there is no market for seeds due to the lack of official approval of old grain varieties (formally it is actually illegal to market them). Furthermore, cultivating old grain varieties requires a change of growing practices, as they respond differently to weeds, fertilizer and soil conditions. In processing, stone-grinding techniques have been introduced as a new and important quality parameter whereby the bran and the germ are retained with the rest of the wheat kernel, which is standard practice in steel-roller mills. The bran and germ are a concentrated source of flavour, essential nutrients and fatty acids, but the fatty acids become rancid less than six months after milling. Consequently stoneground flour has a much shorter shelf life than conventional flour, something which processors, supermarkets and consumers must adapt to. For consumers, specialty flour involves changing kneading and baking practices, as it has a different texture that requires more kneading, higher water content and preferably a sourdough to exploit its full potential.

The emergence of TV-shows promoting baking, cookbooks and baking workshops has introduced this new baking practice to consumers and forged a community of engaged home-bakers.

5.2. Craft beer

Each major Danish city used to have at least one brewery, but since the 1870s, many of these breweries with their local characteristics have been closed, purchased or merged with other breweries, as there is a huge benefit of economies of scale in brewing. By 2002 there were less than 20 registered breweries left, some of which were micro-scale pub breweries and the Danish beer market was dominated by one actor and one beer type, the pilsner.

In the period after 2000 a dramatic development began to take place, allegedly initiated with a beer festival in Copenhagen, where the writer and journalist Michael Jackson made a pledge for a beer revolution:

> Never before has Copenhagen seen such a selection of beers under one roof. Explore them, savour the flavours of great and distinctive brews, and you will never ask for 'a beer' again. It is never too late to join the revolution.

Subsequently Danes slowly acquired a taste for imported specialty brew (a market share of around 3% in 2002), and the opening of a few brewpubs demonstrated that craft beer had a marketing potential. Interestingly, it was Carlsberg, the giant Danish multinational brewery, that took the first steps in the new development with a popular marketing stunt in 1997 conducting a national beer referendum that introduced a range of beer types, which were previously unknown to the general public. This illustrates the complex relationship between niche and mainstream. The development is also seen in the number of new beer types introduced to the market. In 1999, 17 new beers were introduced to the Danish market; in 2014 this figure had increased to 1108 new beers and the market share of craft beer had increased to 15%.

Craft breweries are a diverse group of companies that are often small breweries using traditional techniques, craftsmanship and that interpret historic styles with unique twists to develop new styles. According to our interviewees, craft brewers have adopted different business strategies, where three distinct forms were identified by the interviewees. First, a group of breweries have focused on 'extreme brewing' or 'gourmet beer', oriented towards the international specialty market or local gourmet restaurants and brewpubs (e.g. Mikkeller, Evil Twin and To øl). In this market it is important to stand out and the companies have adopted a boundary-pushing strategy, exemplified by the Mikkeller beer 'Beer Geek Brunch Weasel' – a stout brewed with civet coffee (part-digested coffee cherries eaten and defecated by a weasel-like civet cats). Many of these companies do not have their own brewery, but work as 'gypsy brewers', developing recipes and branding, but contract the actual brewing out to other companies. Second, a group of breweries have focused on brewing various types of craft beers for Danish supermarkets (e.g. Ørbæk, Svaneke Bryghus and Rise Bryggeri). In this market, products are sold in bulk; so it is important to brew a range of different beer types that fulfil the quality expectations in that particular category. Third, another range of breweries have focused strictly on a local market, often combining a brewery with a restaurant or a pub (e.g. Søgaards Bryghus, Bryghuset Vendia or Viborg Bryghus). Furthermore, some of these companies are also owned locally by smallholders and they cater for a local market, fulfilling the expectations of the local market by producing well-known beer types that do not stick out in any way.

Following the financial crisis in 2008 some of the breweries went bankrupt, others were sold or merged, but new companies also emerged and, according to our interviewees, the craft breweries have gradually become more professional during the past 10 years; one of the brewers for instance notes:

> there is increasing focus on product quality [...] more and more measurements, more and more knowledge, it has to be better and better. Eight years ago I visited another brewery, they did not have a brewer, so the owner brewed and the beer was horrid, but it didn't matter, because it sold well at that time.

Furthermore, brewers are no longer only focused on the small community of beer geeks, but have also begun to produce beers for the general public. As a result, the ales that have dominated the specialty market are supplemented with pilsner and weissbier.

According to one of the first craft brewers, the brewing world is characterized by a collaborative culture and brewers are very open towards sharing knowledge and skills. A brewer describes this: 'rather than a world where people are constantly on their guard, a cooperative culture has been created'. However, there is also pronounced competition among the different brewers; this is driven by a desire to brew 'the best' beer, recognized by the community of beer appreciators. These are two important drivers of the development, as focus is given to continuous improvements of taste and uniqueness.

The Danish craft brewers have diverse backgrounds; some have been conventionally educated and have a background with major brewing companies, but many craft brewers do not. This combination of 'professionals' and engaged 'amateurs' has proved to be a successful combination and one of the interviewees without a formal brewing background notes:

> If you are formally trained you become very good at a lot of things, but you also wear blinkers; by learning via websites, books and other microbrewers you learn something much more practical; a formally trained brewer would know which amino acids do so and so during brewing; I can tell you if it tastes good, and if it does I will use it in my beer.

It is emphasized that the newcomers enter the craft beer world with a completely different view on beer quality, devoid of the conventions that follow from formal training and with an engagement towards the production of a different version of beer.

Hence, the quality conventions that have characterized beer have gradually been transformed. In particular, the 'extreme brewers' have pushed the boundaries by introducing a range of new flavours, and suddenly craft beers are reviewed in magazines, celebrated at brewpubs and beer festivals – a new beer culture has emerged. Furthermore, the pilsner has gradually been replaced by new beer types and beer has changed role, replacing wine as an accompaniment to good food. However, even the craft beer sector relies on the same ingredients as the multinational companies and there are only a handful of malting companies and hop producers in Europe that supply the raw material, although this is currently also in transition and a few new companies have begun the production of hops and malt.

5.3. Organic broilers

The Danish organic broiler production began in the mid-1990s and increased dramatically up until 2001 where the annual production peaked at around 500,000 broilers. However, by 2007 the production was reduced to less than 50,000 as marketing efforts were lacking, it was difficult to obtain the substantial price premium that was needed and there was an unstable demand in the processing industry. Furthermore, the production system experienced problems with coccidiosis, which was made worse by the regulation imposed to prevent avian flu that restricted outdoor rearing.

The organic production regulation has been adopted from the French Label Rouge system that specifies slow-growing genotypes, a higher slaughtering age (81–110 days), small herd size (4800), more space allocated per chicken (4 m^2) and a smaller daily weight gain (<35 g), which make the production costly. In 2007 the regulation was altered (in practice watered down) to reduce the costs of organic broiler production by enabling a lower slaughtering age (principally no restriction if the parent stock of slow-growing breeds is organic), faster-growing genotypes and coccidiosis vaccination (Hermansen, Horsted, & Kongsted, 2014). At the same time, the large-scale abattoir Rose Poultry began producing organic broilers. The production has, once again, increased to above 500,000 in 2014, but the market share of organic broilers is still less than 1% (DST, 2015).

A new development began in the spring of 2015, when the largest discount supermarket chain, Netto, introduced the French Label Rouge broiler to Danish consumers, which is acclaimed for its high animal welfare and superior taste. Furthermore, the small-scale abattoir Sødam began producing 'welfare broilers' for another supermarket chain, COOP, which is similar to the organic broiler apart from the feed. These products have become a huge success and the French Label Rouge broilers has become the preferred choice among the customers in Netto, despite the price being three times higher (Haar, 2016).

Generally, broilers are perceived as a cheap and lean meat product that is easy to prepare, therefore it has become an important ingredient in quickly prepared everyday meals. Differentiations in the product category include various brands, cuts and marinades, but there is little variation in the primary production. According to the manager of one of the broiler processing companies, animal welfare is the most important criterion for consumers:

> The reason that consumers choose organic chickens is not simply because of the label, it is primarily because they care about animal welfare […] but we hope that it [introduction of Label Rouge and welfare broilers] can also boost our organic sales.

Furthermore, the price for an organic broiler is perceived to be a large barrier to developing the organic broiler market. One of the issues is that organic broilers are caught in the catch-22 situation whereby prices are high because volumes are low and volumes are low because prices are high. Furthermore, according to several actors in the food system, there is simply too little variation in the product category to make it exciting for consumers, as engaged consumer request a differentiated selection (Thorsøe et al., 2015). It would be possible to differentiate the organic broiler in a number of ways – by age, feed, weight, sex and breed. This would disassociate the organic broiler from cheap everyday food, but so far no one has adopted a differentiation strategy.

The abattoirs are an important link for organic broiler production (Thorsøe et al., 2015). However, abattoirs do not find the attributes that are related to organic production entirely positive. For instance, variation in weight and the heterogeneity of organic broilers, due to outdoor rearing, are difficult to manage in an industrial production. Furthermore, the abattoirs are large production units and the organic production lots are smaller, which makes slaughtering costs of these broilers higher. Selling organic broilers as frozen food would, to some extent, alleviate the problem by allowing larger quantities in one batch rather than a continuous small-scale supply, thereby lowering the abattoir costs. However, the quality conventions in the Danish broiler market dictate fresh meat only as the retail sector prefer customers who purchase fresh produce, as fresh produce carries a higher price premium and customers who prefer fresh produce frequent the shops more often, thus purchasing more in total. Furthermore, customers who purchase frozen food are perceived as more parsimonious, and thus as unattractive customers for supermarkets. Therefore the retail sector has gradually removed frozen food from their product range in favour of fresh food.

Until recently, the organic broiler production has not been financially viable for abattoirs, but the production has been retained due to strategic considerations. The interviewees emphasized that small differences in marginal costs determine profitability. In consequence, the abattoirs cut up the broilers and sell each part in different markets where the prices are highest. It is not possible to obtain an organic price premium for broiler feet (a high-value product for the abattoir) because they are consumed in Asia, where there is currently no organic market. According to the manager of one of the lager abattoirs, this has been problematic for their business model.

Small-scale organic broiler production is further challenged by the veterinary regulation which is adapted to conventional production. All types of salmonella are for instance prohibited, even though they are not all harmful, which is problematic since they are difficult to avoid in outdoor rearing. In addition, abattoirs must perform costly veterinary control inspections that greatly influence the start-up and running costs of the units and function as a barrier for small-scale production.

6. Discussion

In this section we will initially compare the three case studies to identify differences and similarities in terms of how the new food conventions are expressed. Secondly, we will explore what influences if and how new food trends are expressed in the food system.

6.1. Comparison of the case studies

The three cases display a different relationship with organic production (see Table 1). The development of old grain varieties and specialty flour is strongly motivated by organic producers, who aspire to develop grain varieties that are better adapted to organic production and hence attempt to push the boundaries of organic production. Taste is the main driver for producers in the craft beer category, and whether or not ingredients are organic is of secondary importance. Furthermore, there is only a limited organic production of malt and hops; hence it is difficult to produce organic beer. Production of organic broilers is based on common guidelines collaboratively developed by the food system actors.

Locality and origin are prominent aspects within specialty flour and craft beer, but it is not a tendency that is expressed much in organic broilers. This indicates two different understandings of product quality: one that emphasizes uniqueness and diversity such as represented by craft beer and specialty and another that emphasizes standards and uniformity as represented by organic broilers.

Emphasizing a difference in taste has been an important aspect in the development of old grain varieties and craft beer, but this quality aspect is completely absent in organic broilers, as they are not designed or marketed as a different taste experience compared with their conventional counterpart. Hence, one of the challenges of the organic broiler industry may be their emphasis on ethical qualities, particularly animal welfare. The successful introduction of the French Label Rouge broiler to Netto may be an early warning that organic production may be overtaken by other production systems that also emphasize aesthetic qualities.

In the specialty flour and craft beer product categories, building a community around the products and embedding new experiences into the products is a critical innovation, not only in the product categories but in the Danish foodscape. This expression of community and experience is not seen with organic broilers.

Table 1. The table details how the four tendencies outlined in Section 3 are translated in each product category.

	Specialty flour	Craft beer	Organic broilers
Organics	The development of old grain varieties was driven by organic farmers in attempts to improve organic production	Few dedicated organic breweries, the majority are non-organic. Poor selection of organic ingredients	The requirements for organic broiler production are gradually adapted to industrial organic production
Locality and origin	Traceability, personal narratives, historical reconnection and grain origin are important aspects of the quality	In labels and brands, beer embrace a particular locality; however, key ingredients are usually not locally produced	Interpreted as Danish products
Taste	Important aspect of product differentiation emphasizing freshness, essential oils, flour and bread texture	Important aspect of product differentiation expressed in new beer types, new ingredients, in reviews, competitions and virtual communities such as Ratebeer.com	Organic broilers are not marketed or differentiated from conventional broilers based on taste, but rather animal welfare attributes
Community and experiences	Development of a new home-baking culture, facilitated by baking courses, food festivals, cookbooks and tv-shows	Development of a new beer culture, facilitated by brewpubs, beer festivals, DIY home brewing and the association 'Danish Beer Enthusiasts'	Not expressed

6.2. Expressing food trends in the product categories

Based on the above comparison, we argue that there are at least three important lessons to be learnt from the case studies and how qualities have been developed within each.

6.2.1. Translating the food trends

Focusing on conventions emphasizes the different modes whereby qualities are valuated in the food system and the relationship between the food system and general concerns in society (Boltanski & Thevenot, 2006). Hence, the food trends are not invented by particular producers alone, but producers may attempt to relate their products to these conventions. The case studies also indicate that conventions need to be translated and embedded in each product category and this is a complex social process. For instance, the interpretation of 'local' – which is important in all case studies but differs quite a lot – in specialty flour refers to where the grains have been grown and where they have been processed; in craft beer local only refers to the place of production, and in organic chickens to products from Denmark. Hence, the case studies indicate that food trends do not presuppose one particular interpretation and implementation in each product category, but the quality conventions may be interpreted in a number of different ways. Furthermore, also across different countries there are differences in how the conventions of specialty foods are implemented (Halkier, 2017). The product categories that we have compared in this analysis are only related inasmuch as they sometimes draw on the same cultural codes. This indicates that the food trends need to be seen as potentials that may or may not find a concrete expression in particular products. This in line with Moragues-Faus and Sonnino (2012) and Tregear (2011), who support the need for a focus on the wider socio-economic and territorial context in which the food system is embedded to understand the emergence of new food qualities.

6.2.2. Embedding new quality aspects in the food system

In line with Marsden and Smith (2005), we find that the success of the new alternative food networks is conditioned by their ability to radically distance themselves from intensively based production systems. Furthermore, as also noted by Stræte (2008), the case studies explored in this article demonstrate that enabling new modes of production require a mobilization of a new food system or the enrolment of new actors who are able to understand and rethink consumer engagement, competencies and roles. However, if producers are able to do this, then there is a great transformative potential, as also noted by Brunori, Rossi, and Guidi (2012). We find that this is particularly true if producers are able to combine different quality aspects into a particular product, such as ethical concerns related to production and processing with aesthetical aspects such as taste. Furthermore, enabling new modes of engaging consumers and building a culture around the products is a fundamental requirement for producers to successfully enable new modes of production.

The focus on taste has also altered how products are marketed as supermarkets have altered their address to the consumers of craft beer and specialty flour. They are no longer addressed as 'an economic man', but rather as 'foodies', engaged consumers who are willing to pay a substantial price premium for a specialty product, where a range of different qualities are emphasized (Johnston & Baumann, 2010). The engaged foodie requires differentiated products to fulfil particular needs, such as a 'beer to go with a pork roast' rather than just 'a beer', or 'flour to make ciabatta bread' rather than just 'flour'. Hence, there is not one product in each category capable of fulfilling all needs of everybody at the same time.

Community and experience are needed for consumers to acquire the skills that are essential to appreciate the new products. For instance, consumers of specialty flour need to change their baking practice; otherwise old grain varieties will not be seen as an improvement, but rather as a nuisance. The cases of craft beer and specialty flour demonstrate that a 'community of appreciators' is a critical success factor. These communities engage consumers and facilitate the dissemination of the knowledge and skills that are needed to appreciate the products, and the communities are forged in workshops, festivals, TV-shows and books. By contrast, no such communities are formed around organic broilers, where qualities are only mediated via labelling. However, this culture-building is not only a critical factor for the consumers, but also among producers it has been quite important. For instance the 'DIY (Do It Yourself) mind-set' (the method of doing practical jobs yourself without the direct aid of recognized experts or professionals) and the 'shareware culture' from the IT community is stressed as an important factor for many of the start-ups in the craft beer category.

The transition which has been observed in the craft beer and specialty flour cases has significantly reconfigured the food system, as a range of new actors have been mobilized. This has been observed in other studies, too (Carolan, 2015). A transition is complex and requires an extensive reconfiguration of the food system involving a modification of production techniques, technology and sales channels, diversifying product lines, and consumers must appreciate new taste experiences, preparation techniques, as well as considerably higher prices. In the cases of craft beer and specialty flour, there has been a need for new actors to address the new concerns. Many entrepreneurs, which were drivers of the development in the craft beer and specialty flour categories, had no prior experience in either brewing or milling; therefore they had no formal attachment to the dominating quality conventions. They got engaged as 'amateurs' to produce the best beer or flour in the world with the motivation of revolutionizing the product categories, in accordance with the original meaning of amateurism – doing something for the love of doing it (Teil & Hennion, 2004).

As also noted by, for instance, Sonnino and Marsden (2006) and Stræte and Marsden (2006), there is a complex relationship between the 'alternative' and the 'conventional' food system. The three cases explored in this paper represent three different positions on how food qualities are changing. The specialty flour case illustrates that an 'alternative' food system may function as a laboratory where new ideas are developed and tested and then also become adopted by 'conventional' actors when proven successful. The craft beer case illustrates that the 'conventional' food system may take a more active part in the development of new quality aspects. Furthermore, the organic broiler case demonstrates that the 'conventional' food system may find no interest in a focus on new qualities and may resist a transition because it goes against their operating logic.

In sum, the embedding of new food qualities in the food system is a multidimensional reconfiguration, involving a number of changes, including particular dynamics within commodity types, but also cultural processes that are common to all commodity types, structural changes in the retail sector, such as the advent of new wholesalers emphasizing products with added value and providing market access for small- and medium-sized producers and structural changes in production and new product development.

6.2.3. The challenge of incompatible logics

Based on the case studies, it is our contention that a differentiated selection of products within each commodity type is one of the fundamental bases for engaging consumers and building a culture around the product categories. A differentiated selection allows consumers to develop preferences, adopt and display skills. This is also seen in other product categories that offer a diverse selection such as wine or cheese (Krzywoszynska, 2015). The 'conventional' food system is organized around standardized products, implying predefined generic qualities and a disembedding of the social relations in the value chain (Busch, 2011). However, the specialty flour and craft beer cases are distinguished by a diverse range of qualities, which is a good basis for engaging consumers, suggesting that a requirement for expressing the new food trends is a break with the logic of standardization.

A transition not only requires a change in logic, but also an investment in the transformation. In particular, the specialty flour case demonstrates that when new food qualities are developed the existing food system might not initially appreciate them, and the innovation takes place in spite of the existing food system rather than as a result of its effort and investments. Hence, innovations may be developed and stabilized outside conventional marketing channels by producers who are keen on producing a particular commodity and therefore nurture a market relation capable of transferring this particular commodity. But innovations may also be sustained by consumers who are keen on a particular product and therefore find alternative ways of addressing this demand, as illustrated in a case study on the diversification of the Danish organic market (Thorsøe & Noe, 2016).

Cost reduction is the principal way of gaining a comparative advantage in the food system. This article, along with the work of a range of different scholars, documents that there is another way of prevailing in a competitive market that goes against the dominating trend of reducing costs, by instead adding value (Renting et al., 2003; Stræte & Marsden, 2006). This may be done by emphasizing a range of new quality aspects that have not previously been associated with these categories, whereby producers are able to short-circuit this zero-sum game in a way that increases the total amount of money spent on the product category. In fact, within the craft beer and specialty flour sector, consumers now spend a much larger proportion of their total spending on food in these categories. This benefits not only the new actors, but also a number of the established actors; for instance, the share of discount beer has declined and many producers have begun producing mid-range and expensive beers as the share of these has increased. Within craft beer and specialty flour, much more value has been added than anybody imagined when they set out to revolutionize the product categories. This suggests that there is a great potential for rearranging the food system by adding value, although it requires a break with the implicit logic that still governs many product categories, including organic chickens – but it's never too late to join the revolution!

7. Conclusions

In this paper we have explored, what influences if and how new food trends are expressed in the food system. The article documents that new products are constructed by particular producers interpreting, embedding and justifying their products by reference to a number of prevailing food trends. The food trends are not the invention of the individual producer, but serve as a common convention that products can be related to and it is not pre-given how they should be interpreted. Furthermore, the study demonstrates that the revolution is not taking place in just the one domain, but it implies a multidimensional reconfiguration of the food system, including changing the operating logic, structural changes, enrolling new actors, enabling new modes of consumer engagement and a product culture. Furthermore, a transition of the food system presupposes a shared vision and a coordination of activities among the actors in the food system or the mobilization of new actors who share this vision. A critical factor is a diversification of the product category; focusing on multiple quality aspects, the analysis documents that doing so may benefit the product category as a whole by attracting a higher share of consumers' money.

By conducting a comparative case study, we further demonstrated how a particular quality convention is expressed in different product categories that are not otherwise related. Hence, food qualities are embedded in a wider socio-material context and the reduction of this context to simple categories such as sensory characteristics, preferences or labelling and communication will not capture the complexity of a transition. Adopting a CT perspective offers a way to conceptualize changes that are not economic, but have implications for how the economy is shaped and organized. Hence, in line with Rosin and Campbell (2009), we find that adopting a CT perspective enables a processual view of emphasizing the contested, incremental and potentially rapid evolution of food system change.

Disclosure statement

No potential conflict of interest was reported by the authors.

Funding

This work was carried out in the MultiChick project (j.nr. 34009-13-0690) funded by the Organic RDD-2 program under the Green Development- and demonstration program (GUDP under The Ministry of Environment and Food of Denmark), coordinated by The International Centre for Research in Organic Food Systems (ICROFS).

References

Barnett, C. (2014). Geography and ethics III: From moral geographies to geographies of worth. *Progress in Human Geography, 38*(1), 151–160. doi:10.1177/0309132513514708

Bernzen, A., & Braun, B. (2014). Conventions in cross-border trade coordination: The case of organic food imports to Germany and Australia. *Environment and Planning A, 46*(5), 1244–1262. doi:10.1068/a46275

Biggart, N. W., & Beamish, T. D. (2003). The economic sociology of conventions: Habit, custom, practice, and routine in market order. *Annual Review of Sociology, 29*, 443–464. doi:10.1146/annurev.soc.29.010202.100051

Boltanski, L., & Thevenot, L. (2006). *On justification: Economies of worth*. Princeton, NJ: Princeton University Press.

Brinkmann, S., & Kvale, S. (2008). *InterViews: Learning the craft of qualitative research interviewing*. Los Angeles, CA: Sage.

Brunori, G., Rossi, A., & Guidi, F. (2012). On the new social relations around and beyond food. Analysing consumers' role and action in Gruppi di Acquisto Solidale (Solidarity Purchasing Groups). *Sociologia Ruralis, 52*(1), 1–30. doi:10.1111/j.1467-9523.2011.00552.x

Busch, L. (2011). *Standards: Recipes for reality*. London: MIT Press.

Byrkjeflot, H., Pedersen, J. S., & Svejenova, S. (2013). From label to practice: The process of creating new Nordic cuisine. *Journal of Culinary Science & Technology, 11*(1), 36–55. doi:10.1080/15428052.2013.754296

Carolan, M. (2015). Re-wilding food systems: Visceralities, utopias, pragmatism, and practice. In P. V. Stock, M. Carolan, & C. Rosin (Eds.), *Food utopias: Reimagining citizenship, ethics and community* (pp. 126–140). London: Routledge.

Carolan, M. S. (2011). *Embodied food politics*. Farnham: Ashgate.

Christensen, T., Olsen, S. B., Kærgård, N., & Dubgaard, A. (2014). *Dokumentation af MultiTrust spørgeskema om økologisk forbrug*. København: Institut for fødevare- og ressourceøkonomi - Københavns Universitet.

Coq-Huelva, D., Sanz-Cañada, J., & Sánchez-Escobar, F. (2014). Conventions, commodity chains and local food systems: Olive oil production in 'Sierra De Segura' (Spain). *Geoforum, 56*, 6–16. doi:10.1016/j.geoforum.2014.06.001

Corbin, J. M. (1998). *Basics of qualitative research: Techniques and procedures for developing grounded theory*. Thousand Oaks, CA: Sage.

DST. (2015). *Statistics Denmark*. Ministry for Economic Affairs and the Interior. Retrieved March 24, 2015, from http://www.statistikbanken.dk/OEKO3

Eriksen, S. N., & Sundbo, J. (2016). Drivers and barriers to the development of local food networks in rural Denmark. *European Urban and Regional Studies, 23*, 750–764. doi:10.1177/0969776414567971

Flyvbjerg, B. (2006). Five misunderstandings about case-study research. *Qualitative Inquiry, 12*(2), 219–245. doi:10.1177/1077800405284363

Geels, F. W. (2004). From sectoral systems of innovation to socio-technical systems. *Research Policy, 33*(6–7), 897–920. doi:10.1016/j.respol.2004.01.015

George, A. L., & Bennett, A. (2005). *Case studies and theory development in the social sciences*. Cambridge: MIT Press.

Goodman, D. (2003). The quality 'turn' and alternative food practices: Reflections and agenda. *Journal of Rural Studies, 19*(1), 1–7. doi:10.1016/S0743-0167(02)00043-8

Haar, S. (2016). *Netto: Salget af fritgående kyllinger slår nu industrikyllingerne*. Politiken.

Halkier. (2017). Quality turns in Nordic food: A comparative analysis of specialty food in Denmark, Norway and Sweden. European Planning Studies.

Hermansen, J. E., Horsted, K., & Kongsted, A. G. (2014). Meat, animal, poultry and fish production and management: Meat production in organic farming. In C. Devine, & M. Dikeman (Eds.), *Encyclopedia of meat sciences* (2nd ed., pp. 199–203). Oxford: Elsevier.

Hermansen, M. E. T. (2012). Creating terroir: An anthropological perspective on new Nordic cuisine as an expression of nordic identity. *Anthropology of Food* (S7). Retrieved from http://aof.revues.org/7249

Hinrichs, C. C., & Allen, P. (2008). Selective patronage and social justice: Local food consumer campaigns in historical context. *Journal of Agricultural and Environmental Ethics, 21*(4), 329–352. doi:10.1007/s10806-008-9089-6

Holm, L., Ekström, M. P., Gronow, J., Kjærnes, U., Lund, T. B., Mäkelä, J., & Niva, M. (2012). The modernisation of Nordic eating: Studying changes and stabilities in eating patterns. *Anthropology of Food* (S7). Retrieved from http://aof.revues.org/6997

Johnston, J., & Baumann, S. (2010). *Foodies: Democracy and distinction in the gourmet foodscape*. London: Routledge.

Kjærnes, U., Harvey, M., & Warde, A. (2007). *Trust in food: A comparative and institutional analysis*. Hampshire: Palgrave Macmillan.

Kjeldsen, C., Kidmose, U., & Kristensen, H. L. (2014). *Terroir: Oprindelse (autenticitet), oprindelsesstedets indflydelse på produktets kvalitet (terroir), samt branding, kvalitetsudvikling, regionale produkter og oprindelsesmærkning*. Tjele: DCA - Nationalt Center for Fødevarer og Jordbrug, Aarhus Universitet.

Krzywoszynska, A. (2015). Wine is not Coca-Cola: Marketization and taste in alternative food networks. *Agriculture and Human Values, 32*(3), 491–503. doi:10.1007/s10460-014-9564-9

Kvam, G.-T., & Bjørkhaug, H. (2013). *Healthy growth: From niche to volume with integrity and trust.* State of the art: National report Norway.

Lund, T. B., Andersen, L. M., & O'Doherty Jensen, K. (2013). The emergence of diverse organic consumers: Does a mature market undermine the search for alternative products? *Sociologia Ruralis, 53*(4), 454–478. doi:10.1111/soru.12022

Mansfield, B. (2003). Spatializing globalization: A 'geography of quality' in the seafood industry. *Economic Geography, 79*(1), 1–16. doi:10.1111/j.1944-8287.2003.tb00199.x

Marsden, T., & Smith, E. (2005). Ecological entrepreneurship: Sustainable development in local communities through quality food production and local branding. *Geoforum, 36*(4), 440–451. doi:10.1016/j.geoforum.2004.07.008

Meldgaard, M., Johansen, P. H., Hjalager, A.-M., Hoff, H., Kjeldsen, C., Thorsøe, M. H., ... Ståhl, E. E. (2015). *Kapitel 8: Erhverv og landdistrikter. Økologiens bidrag til samfundsgoder.* Foulum, DK, ICROFS.

Moragues-Faus, A. M., & Sonnino, R. (2012). Embedding quality in the agro-food system: The dynamics and implications of place-making strategies in the olive oil sector of Alto Palancia, Spain. *Sociologia Ruralis, 52*(2), 215–234. doi:10.1111/j.1467-9523.2011.00558.x

The Nordic Council of Ministers. (2012). *Nordic Council of Ministers.* Retrieved August 21, 2012, from http://nynordiskmad.org

Økodag. (2014). *Økodag.* Organic Association. Retrieved February 2, 2015, from http://okodag.dk

ØL. (2015). *Internal note: Redegørelse for dyrkning af diverse ikke registreret sædekorn.* Aarhus: Økologisk Landsforening.

Ponte, S. (2016). Convention theory in the Anglophone agro-food literature: Past, present and future. *Journal of Rural Studies, 44*, 12–23. doi:10.1016/j.jrurstud.2015.12.019

Ponte, S., & Gibbon, P. (2005). Quality standards, conventions and the governance of global value chains. *Economy and Society, 34*(1), 1–31. doi:10.1080/0308514042000329315

Raynolds, L. T. (2004). The globalization of organic agro-food networks. *World Development, 32*(5), 725–743. doi:10.1016/j.worlddev.2003.11.008

Renard, M.-C. (2005). Quality certification, regulation and power in fair trade. *Journal of Rural Studies, 21*(4), 419–431. doi:10.1016/j.jrurstud.2005.09.002

Renting, H., Marsden, T., & Banks, J. (2003). Understanding alternative food networks: Exploring the role of short food supply chains in rural development. *Environment and Planning A, 35*(3), 393–411. doi:10.1068/a3510

Rosin, C., & Campbell, H. (2009). Beyond bifurcation: Examining the conventions of organic agriculture in New Zealand. *Journal of Rural Studies, 25*(1), 35–47. doi:10.1016/j.jrurstud.2008.05.002

Salais, R., & Storper, M. (1992). The four 'worlds' of contemporary industry. *Cambridge Journal of Economics, 16*(2), 169–193.

Sonnino, R., & Marsden, T. (2006). Beyond the divide: Rethinking relationships between alternative and conventional food networks in Europe. *Journal of Economic Geography, 6*(2), 181–199. doi:10.1093/jeg/lbi006

Stark, D. (2011). *The sense of dissonance: Accounts of worth in economic life.* Princeton: Princeton University Press.

Storper, M., & Salais, R. (1997). *Worlds of production. The action frameworks of the economy.* London: Harvard University Press.

Stræte, E. P. (2008). Modes of qualities in development of speciality food. *British Food Journal, 110*(1), 62–75. doi:10.1108/00070700810844795

Stræte, E. P., & Marsden, T. (2006). Exploring dimensions of qualities in food. In T. Marsden, & J. Murdoch (Eds.), *Between the local and the global: Confronting complexity in the contemporary agri-food sector* (pp. 269–297). Amsterdam: Elsevier.

Teil, G., & Hennion, A. (2004). Discovering quality or performing taste? A sociology of the amateur. In M. Harvey, A. McMeekin, & A. Warde (Eds.), *Qualities of food* (pp. 19–37). Manchester: Manchester University Press.

Thorsøe, M. H. (2015). Maintaining trust and credibility in a continuously evolving organic food system. *Journal of Agricultural and Environmental Ethics, 28*(4), 767–787. doi:10.1007/s10806-015-9559-6

Thorsøe, M. H., & Kjeldsen, C. (2016). The constitution of trust: Function, configuration and generation of trust in alternative food networks. *Sociologia Ruralis, 56*(2), 157–175. doi:10.1111/soru.12082

Thorsøe, M. H., Laursen, K. B., & Noe, E. (2015). *Nye udviklingsveje for afsætning af økologiske kyllinger*. Retrieved from http://orgprints.org/29226/

Thorsøe, M. H., & Noe, E. (2016). Cultivating market relations – Diversification in the Danish organic production sector following market expansion. *Sociologia Ruralis, 56*(3), 331–348. doi:10.1111/soru.12086

Tregear, A. (2011). Progressing knowledge in alternative and local food networks: Critical reflections and a research agenda. *Journal of Rural Studies, 27*(4), 419–430. doi:10.1016/j.jrurstud.2011.06.003

Tregear, A., Arfini, F., Belletti, G., & Marescotti, A. (2007). Regional foods and rural development: The role of product qualification. *Journal of Rural Studies, 23*(1), 12–22. doi:10.1016/j.jrurstud.2006.09.010

Willer, H., & Lernoud, J. (2014). *The World of Organic Agriculture – Statistics and emerging trends 2014*. FiBL-IFOAM Report. Frick, Sch, FiBL and IFOAM. Retrieved from https://www.fibl.org/fileadmin/documents/shop/1636-organic-world-2014.pdf

Storytelling and meal experience concepts

Lena Mossberg and Dorthe Eide

ABSTRACT
The aim of this study is to explore how storytelling with local and regional origin can be used to develop meal experience concepts in restaurants. Focus is on Nordic food from the perspective of the experience economy. The first goal is to analyse the transformation of menus into experience concepts and dining areas into experiencescapes. The second goal is to investigate if storytelling activities in restaurants can lead to destination development. It is also reflected upon if meal experience storytelling in restaurants has implications for consumers' everyday food consumption. Three cases in Sweden and Norway with different storytelling strategies are selected. In all these cases, the stories are unique, the places are linked to the stories and the personnel take part in the storytelling activities. The stories are easy to communicate and easy for the target group to connect to. The menus are linked to the story and are all based on local Nordic food culture and local food products. The menus are set and offered in experiencescapes that in various ways fit the stories. The concepts have contributed to the destinations with more visitors, more collaboration among businesses and increased media attention.

1. Introduction

This study explores how storytelling can be used to develop meal experience concepts in a Nordic food context. Local and regional food has come increasingly into focus in destination development from numerous perspectives, such as place marketing and branding (Du Rand, Heath, & Alberts, 2003; Okumus, Okumus, & McKercher, 2007; Tellström, Gustafsson, & Mossberg, 2006), food festivals for local development (Cavicchi & Santini, 2014), commercialization of local food culture (Tellström, Gustafsson, & Mossberg, 2005), food and sense of place (Lund, 2015) and food influences on tourists' experience of a destination (Kivela & Crotts, 2006). A perspective that has received limited attention so far is implications of the experience economy for local and regional food in destination development. An exception is the study of Manniche and Larsen (2012) that focuses on how collaboration among small Danish enterprises offering culinary products can be stimulated by experience dimensions.

Experiences as economic offerings follow another logic compared to goods and services. When the consumer pays for an experience-related offering, the person likes to co-create and spend time enjoying events that a company stages (Pine & Gilmore, 1999). With a particular interest in the experience economy in the Nordic countries many companies, organizations and destinations in 'the North' have become inspired to develop new meal experience concepts in order to increase their attractiveness and reach experience-seeking consumers. The development has been facilitated by national and regional programmes on experiences with participants from universities, official authorities and private organizations. Regional tourist boards and regional producer networks have been inspired by the programmes which can be seen in their place-branding activities.

The experience economy perspective presumes that the consumer seeks amusement, fantasy, arousal, sensory stimulation, enjoyment (Holbrook & Hirschman, 1982) and food for fun (de la Ville, Brougère, & Boireau, 2010). Consumers with high involvement in food activities in everyday life (e.g. eating out, experimenting and cooking, collecting cook books) are proposed to build their identity around food (Andersson & Mossberg, 2014; Shenoy, 2005). Activities are selected to display their tastes and differences to others (Warde & Martens, 2000). This experience trend parallels the sustainability trend including health and moral aspects of what we eat. In general, consumers gain power in buying and using food and they have a higher awareness of animal well-being, safety, traceability, local produce and local–global power relations in food provision (Solér, 2012; Spaargaren, Oosterveer, Loeber, &, 2012). These quality dimensions can be perceived as alternative to the traditional view of industrial food production which mostly are focused on price and efficiency (Manniche & Larsen, 2012). Spaargaren (2011) discusses sustainable food consumption and 'ecological modernization' and argues that frequent and intense sustainability-related interaction rituals will increase consumers' commitment and awareness of such phenomenon (p. 816). Sustainable consumption patterns are seen as a result of innovations in practices. In the experience economy literature, it is stated, 'It is the revisiting of a recurring theme, experienced through distinct and yet unified events, that transforms' (Pine & Gilmore, 2013, p. 40). We can therefore assume that intense sustainability-related interaction rituals as well as intense experience-related interaction rituals can change food consumption patterns. We suggest that restaurants trying to involve consumers and following new trends can 'carry along the flows of emotional energies' (Spaargaren, 2011, p. 820) both attached to sustainable and experiential consumption and thereby be part of a transformation process. Story, Kaphingst, Robinson-O'Brien, and Glanz (2008) propose that information about the meals in restaurants can increase consumer awareness and stimulate demand for more healthful choices. Despite there are several models for policies in restaurants to increase healthier eating, there has not been a systematic evaluation, according to them. We think there is a need to find out more about how restaurants correspond to these trends with innovative offerings.

The changes in food production as well as in food consumption have been studied extensively from various disciplines. One characteristic of the experience economy is the integration of production and consumption which clearly emerges in the two main theoretical frameworks within experiential marketing: experience staging and experience consumption. Experience staging has been developed from a marketing management perspective focusing on how to create new experiences (Pine & Gilmore, 1999, 2013). It holds a business-oriented perspective on how to engage and involve consumers for them to be immersed in the experience. The seminal article by Arnould and Price (1993) is an example of the other framework on experience consumption. Consumer culture theory with particular focus on consumer interactions has dominated this debate (Arnould & Thompson, 2005). When Manniche and Larsen (2012) discuss efforts of developing narrative add-ons to food products they suggest experience staging as an overall explanatory framework for value creation in the new food economy. We have also used experience staging as a framework but integrate findings from consumer studies to better understand visitors' consumption in specific themed contexts, which has been asked for (Snel, 2011).

In experience staging the symbolic, aesthetic and hedonic nature of experiences is emphasized as well as consumers' engagement and their search for value creation. One way to engage consumers is to combine storytelling and local food to stage an attractive experiencescape (Mossberg, 2008). With an experiential view, the combination is not remarkable since food is part of a symbolic environment, which can add to the story. Food, according to Bessie're (1998), stimulates the imagination and concentrated symbolic virtues; food is a sign of communion, a class marker and an emblem (culture heritage of a given geographical area). The experiencescape is also symbolic – a commercial place where narratives are negotiated, shaped and transformed through the interaction between producers and consumers (Chronis, 2005). It is a space of pleasure, enjoyment and entertainment, where interactions between people take place (O'Dell & Billing, 2005) and can be described as an 'enchanted zone' (Gustafsson, 2002, pp. 131, 267). Thus, our attention turns towards how powerful stories can transport consumers into imaginary worlds.

One of the most well-known restaurants (experiencescapes) is Noma in Copenhagen, which has had an important role in creating stories and spreading the new Nordic cuisine concept. Noma's international recognition has resulted in many food events with the global gastronomic elite, a great number of TV shows on the concept and a lot of media attention (Sundbo, Sundbo, & Jacobsen, 2013). Therkelsen (2016) studied whether the communication of the new Nordic cuisine has affected the demand for it among German tourists visiting Denmark. She found that the new Nordic cuisine was not established in German coastal tourists mind set. She suggests a linkage between new Nordic cuisine and the food culture of the destinations in focus. The present study follows her suggestions and look into how a destination's food culture and typical meals can be communicated to establish a sense of place.

There are many examples of how stories frame the experiencescape in a restaurant context (Mossberg, 2008). A story is built on common fundamental elements in dramaturgy. A story creates context and simplifies and can give extra meaning to the consumer's experience (Van Laer, de Ruyter, Visconti, & Wetzels, 2014). Restaurants often change their concepts and it is hard to predict whether a storytelling approach will be a failure or a success.

The aim of this study is to explore how storytelling with local and regional origin can be used to develop meal experience concepts in restaurants. Our first goal is to analyse the transformation of menus into experience concepts and dining areas into experiencescapes. The second goal is to investigate if storytelling activities in restaurants can lead to destination development. In addition, we reflect upon the possible implications of our findings regarding meal experience storytelling for consumers' everyday food consumption.

Highlighting storytelling strategies in this study enable us to concentrate on issues of success, sustainability and how to engage the consumers in a restaurant context. The discussion contributes to the debate on experience staging and storytelling in restaurants, how storytelling can make sense and how cultural, geographical and sustainability links are tied together by a story. The study also contributes to the debate on food and local economy and how restaurants can be an agency of change when it comes to daily food consumption. The discussion is based on two cases in Sweden and one in Norway, where storytelling is prominent but used in various ways.

2. Theoretical framework

From a consumer perspective, an experience can be defined as the mental impact felt and remembered by an individual and caused by the personal perception of external stimuli (Sundbo & Sørensen, 2013), such as design, light, scent and sound. Carù and Cova (2007) argue that in staging experiences, special attention should be given to multisensorial stimulation, consumer participation and the story. A model developed in line with these thoughts departs from consumer experiences and marketing and begins with the idea of the experience as a process (Mossberg, 2007). In restaurants, consumers interact with the personnel, the food, other consumers and the experiencescape in the situation. All the parts are also influenced by a story or theme, often connected with the brand (Mossberg, 2008). This can be seen, for example, in restaurants such as Hard Rock Café; the story influences not only the meal but also the interior design, the music, the ways staff are dressed and so on. In this way of thinking, experience is an active appropriation of the world and receptive sensory engagement. The experience does not belong to an individual; it is not located in the human being but rather in interactions with the environment, situation and events (Svabo, Larsen, Haldrup, & Berenholdt, 2013). A place is co-practised co-created, co-performed and generated in interactions, as shown in a number of consumer studies on commercial experiencescapes (Badot & Filser, 2007; Gottdiener, 1998; Hollenbeck, Peters, & Zinkhan, 2008; Kozinets et al., 2002; Peñaloza, 1999; Sherry et al., 2004). An experience is a blend of many elements coming together and if the company succeeds in communicating a good story, consumers might become involved and want to join in and create the experience for themselves.

An earlier study within the Nordic countries explored the possibilities and drawbacks of using storytelling as a means of developing and marketing tourism destinations (Mossberg, Therkelsen, Björk, Huijbens, & Olsson, 2010). The authors created a theoretical model that gave an understanding of destinations as laced with stories. They also showed how stories can form constituent parts in a long-term, multi-actor and multi-level process of destination marketing where all stakeholders and all activities have to be in tune with the storyline.

Storytelling and marketing have been of growing interest, with studies focusing on, for example, branding (Woodside, 2010), advertising (Escalas, 2004), marketing relationships (Stern, Thompson, & Arnould, 1998), consumption (Shankar, Elliot, & Goulding, 2001), marketing communication in general (Pattersson & Brown, 2005), narrated incidents (Guber, 2007), word of mouth (Delgadillo & Escalas, 2004) and consumer experiences (Mossberg, 2008). One prerequisite for the consumer to be immersed during commercial experiences is that there must be a theme (Carù & Cova, 2007) or a story (Hansen & Mossberg, 2013). A story is based on common fundamental elements in dramaturgy, such as message, conflict, division of roles and action (Stern et al., 1998). A concept built on a story has a point to make, a script, often characters, and a sequence in which the story is told (Mossberg, 2008). A story creates meaning but only if the consumer can make acquaintance with and understand the story and also feel part of it. Whether consumers are carried away by a story depends on if they empathize with the story characters and if the story plot activates their imagination (Van Laer et al., 2014). In general, consumers produce different meanings and identities that they want to act out and experience (Firat & Dholakia, 1998). There must be room for the consumer to personally be able to influence the details of the story and to co-create a unique value.

A second prerequisite, according to Carù and Cova (2007), is the presence of an enclave which must contrast with their everyday life. The experience must be out of the ordinary. The consumers take a temporary excursion to an out-of-the-ordinary environment and step into an experiencescape (Quan & Wang, 2004). In this enclave, functional and emotional attributes play an important role (Kumar & Karande, 2000) and costumes, artefacts, brochures and so on are often framed by the story. Within the experiencescape, the consumer has the opportunity to 'act out', interact with and experience new things and forget everyday concerns for a moment. The tourists consume with the help of the guide/personnel (Crang, 1997), who weave episodes and facts into the overall story. They inform, help and sometimes train the consumer to find their way around, and act in, the new surroundings.

The third prerequisite, proposed by Carù and Cova (2007), is safety. The experiences can be exciting, challenging and consist of unusual activities, but the consumers must feel safe and comfortable in their role. Otherwise, they get distracted and cannot fully direct all their attention to the activity and will therefore fail to become immersed in the situation.

3. Methodology

This empirical study is situated within an interpretive–constructionist paradigm, using a hermeneutical approach and multi-case design (Flyvbjerg, 2001). The studied cases are: Astrid Lindgren's World (a theme park in Vimmerby, Sweden); the regional museum in Skara, Sweden and its book tourism project Arn; and Thon Hotel Lofoten (a conference hotel in Lofoten, Norway). The cases were selected for four main reasons: First, they are all based on a main story but their design differs considerably. Second, inter-organizational cooperation has increased the attractiveness not only of the experience concept and the organization but also of the destination, and the case organization has played a central role. Third, the concepts involve Nordic culinary traditions and local food products. Fourth, the cases are situated in Nordic countries and in rural areas. We use a spiral case design and our main case level is the organization, but we also move between different analytical levels (experience concept/organization/destination. Gherardi suggests using a spiral case when needing to move between analytical levels, in order to be able 'to move within the texture of practices from any point of entry' (Gherardi, 2012, p. 173).

Data were gathered through a combination of methods, that is, participative observations and conversations in the field; semi- and unstructured interviews (during meetings); and gathering of documents (newspaper articles, web information, etc.). The Norwegian case has been studied on several occasions and includes longitudinal and more extensive data, while the others were studied mainly during one field trip. Interviews were recorded and transcribed. Following the advice of Krizaj, Brodnik, and Bukovec

Table 1. Main sources of data and methods.

Case	Interviews	Observations	Documents/Internet
Astrid Lindgren's World	Interviews with the CEO, one member of the serving staff and three tourists.	Participant observation and guided tour of the park over two days, including two meals (August 2010).	Internet, magazines and newspaper articles
The regional museum and Arn	Interviews with the marketing director (museum), an Arn guide, a director of a tourist office, four entrepreneurs running restaurants/cafés and a priest. Some follow-ups by mail.	Participant observation during guided tour during four meals related to the Arn concept as well as visits to one museum, two churches, the ruins of a monastery, a park and other sites (August 2010).	Internet, reports, research and newspaper articles
Thon Hotel Lofoten	Interviews with the CEO, two chefs, a freelance artist and six international customers. A CEO in a small local firm producing local food; a manager in a local nature-based experience firm. (1) a consultant; a representative from the regional DMO. Other managers and employees active in networks (Innovative Experiences; Winter Lofoten, Pre-Christmas fairy tale; Gastronomic destinations)	Participant observations of experience concepts: Meal show (Lofoten fishery story, 2011 and 2013); Christmas show (2015); The breakfast concept and more general observations within and across the firms in different occasions, including during formal and informal networks/relations.	Internet, magazines, newspaper articles and two student theses

Note: DMO, destination management organization.

(2014), we engaged a mixed group of stakeholders as informants in interviews and conversations during observations. The informant selection criteria were: (1) people in the organization or in other organizations at the destination involved in production or consumption and (2) different types of stakeholders, that is, not only managers involved in innovations and production. Table 1 gives an overview of the data and informants.

The three cases were first analysed within cases and then across cases. The main method used was content analysis (Miles & Huberman, 1984) using the field and interview guides as a starting point. Each case was also analysed by means of a more open approach but guided by the Five Aspects Meal Model (Gustafsson, Öström, Johansson, & Mossberg, 2006), with a particular focus on the product (the menu) and the room (experiencescape) complemented by the consumer experience model (Mossberg, 2007). In this model the consumption is seen as non-ordinary in contrast to consumers' everyday life.

4. Findings

4.1. Astrid Lindgren's World and the culinary experience

Case number one, Astrid Lindgren's World in Vimmerby, Sweden, is a theme park where visitors can experience characters and stories from Astrid Lindgren's books. The park receives some 450,000 visitors every year, of whom around 30% come from abroad. During the peak season, Astrid Lindgren's World has approximately 360 employees, just over 100 of whom work on the theatrical side. The park's target group used to be families but has now changed to children (the parents come anyway). All activities, restaurants, bathrooms, benches, walkways and so on are built to suit children. The park management decided some years ago to drastically change the type of food served as it is stated that food is an important aspect of the total experience at Astrid Lindgren's World. They removed fast food such as hamburgers, hot dogs and french fries from the menus and replaced nearly all pre- and semi-manufactured food products with authentic, home-cooked Swedish food made from locally produced ingredients. They pointed out for all the involved actors and personnel that sustainability is important and children should eat good and nutritious food. To be able to offer visitors an authentic, healthy culinary experience, but also to support local trade and reduce food miles, the park initiated collaboration with celebrity chefs and local pig farms, potato farms and a local dairy.

The areas in the park are inspired by the books (most of which were published in the 1950s), and the restaurants and menus also fit this time period. Some of Lindgren's books have their own theme restaurants. Examples include Larsson's bakery on Troublemaker Street (designed as a 1950s café). Next to Karlsson's house is Pysslingglass ice cream, inspired by Lindgren's character Karlsson-on-the-Roof. There are also themed restaurants like Hamnmagasinet at Pippi's. One restaurant has a pancake machine with a recipe for Pippi pancakes. The menus are designed with children in mind. In Astrid Lindgren's books there are descriptions of the characters eating pancakes, 'isterband' (a type of sausage), 'kroppkakor' (a potato dish) and meatballs as these dishes are typical for the region. The idea is that these traditional dishes described in the books should be served in the park. Some dishes are also named after the characters, such as Pippi ice cream. All brand names are out of sight for the visitors. A common brand of ice cream is sold but the ice cream boxes are redesigned with a neutral surface.

The change in the park's overall food strategy resulted in ample media attention illustrating and describing the positive effects of the new direction taken. In fact, it has been pointed out as one of the most innovative and good examples of a sustainable food concept related to tourism in Sweden.

4.2. Arn and the culinary experience

The regional museum in Skara, Sweden has been the central coordinator of activities related to the story of Arn Magnusson. Arn is a fictional medieval knight and crusader from the highly successful Arn trilogy, a series of novels written by Swedish author Jan Guillou. The stories have been made into films, TV series and TV documentaries and have also resulted in book- and film-based tourism. Travelling in Arn's footsteps is one way to bring the fictional tale and the factual history together in one destination. In the best year, the various Arn spots attracted more than 400,000 visitors.

During the Arn era (interest has cooled down considerably now), tourists could visit cafés and restaurants while touring churches, monasteries and so on mentioned in the Arn books. They could also visit man-made attractions based on the films. Forshems Gästgiveri, with a neighbouring medieval church mentioned in the books, has offered food and drinks to visitors for hundreds of years. The restaurant is decorated according to local history without any connection to medieval time. It is certified as a slow-food restaurant and is also quality certified by the West Sweden Tourist Board in its Taste of West Sweden programme. One meal experience concept was the so-called Arn menu, which targeted bus tourists. For the restaurant, the concept was easy to handle. It was possible to serve many guests at the same time and also many guests in one day without losing quality. The Arn menu consisted of a main course with minced deer meat from the area, roasted and boiled vegetables, and gravy. Coffee and cake were served for dessert. The serving staff always presented the menu to all visitors, they were able to link it to the Arn story and integrate the meal with the tourists' overall historical experience.

One café is located near another church linked to the Arn story. That visitors could sometimes watch, for example, a sword being made is another element of the experience concept besides the location. The main element, however, was the Arn cake, which the owner developed with a secret recipe in order to attract visitors. The development consisted of re-naming a traditional popular type of Swedish cake to 'Arn cake'. Because of this cake, the café got involved in the Arn tours and brochures and attracted a lot of bus tourists and individual visitors every week. Both the Arn menu and the Arn cake were quality certified by the Arn Academy, which was coordinated by the regional museum and consisted of the tourist managers in the local tourism organizations at the destination.

The interest in Arn that followed the trilogy has now lost a lot of the momentum it once had; yet, it added colour to the destination for many years. No one could ever have expected the great interest the books and films raised for visits to the area. New organizations started, new collaborations among organizations were launched and new Arn concepts and products were developed, distributed and sold. Researchers from various disciplines became interested in the phenomenon, municipalities were fighting to be part of the activities, local museums got new ideas, a theme park opened, tourneys were arranged, there were performances by local theatre groups and the regional museum could see a major increase in people's interest in the medieval times, in particular among school children. The Arn meals strengthened the overall consumer experience and could be seen as an added value. The success of the restaurants and other firms linking to the Arn story was partly a result of their own ideas and work, but they could not have done it alone. Instead, they were totally dependent on the Arn story, how the Arn project was organized as a network of private and public stakeholders and how it was coordinated and quality controlled.

4.3. Thon hotel in Svolvaer and the culinary experience

The hotel is located in Svolvær, a fishing village in Lofoten, Norway. The nature, culture and not least the history related to fishing attract a large number of national and international tourists. The hotel opened in March 2009, has about 140 employees, almost 200 hotel rooms, conference rooms, a restaurant, a bar and a pub. The hotel's integration with the local culture centre has led to new meal experience concepts for large groups.

The innovative concepts include various staged and scripted dinner shows arranged throughout the year. One is the Christmas show, which combines a large buffet of local foods with entertainment provided by a theatre group from the area. Both the food and the entertainment vary slightly each year. Moreover, employees entertain in untraditional ways, like when the chefs present and open the meals, serving staff dance and the CEO takes on roles such as a drummer, James Bond or a pirate. Managers are visible hosts and welcome guests at the door and from the stage, as well as roam the floor and talk to guests. Every morning they serve coffee in the breakfast hall. All of this creates a mixture of personalized hospitality, local food products and cultural entertainment. Each Christmas show has room for about 450 guests.

Another dinner show is 'Lofoten', offered year-round to large conference groups. All elements are designed to tell the story about Lofoten in time and space. The show comes with a set menu with four dishes based on local resources and traditions, designed as a tour through the meal. Food is served at the table and in between the courses an artist entertains by telling stories about a fictive Lofoten fisherman. Photos and films portraying different aspects of nature in Lofoten are projected on the walls of the room. Music, light and smoke machines enhance the story and atmosphere. The script is planned down to the second, but still the meal can last about 3–4 hours.

A third meal show concept is 'Polar expedition'. Many of the same design elements from the 'Lofoten' concept are re-used, but food (e.g. fish in tin box), stories, pictures and acting are provided based on the polar expedition story.

The dinner-show concepts have become guest magnets that attract groups from both nearby regions and other parts of the country, sometimes also internationally. The Christmas show takes place in a period that is normally low season, yet it generates traffic and considerable economic value for the hotel and for other firms since visitors often participate in other activities, such as trekking and culture tours. The shows target large conference groups throughout the year. Cooperation is a key word and the hotel depends on many local resources and local food producers for their menus. The hotel has become a hub for interactions, innovations and value creation and has, for example, received an award for 'best event arena in Norway' (2014, by HSMAI). The area has also become attractive to potential employees and to entrepreneurs. Furthermore, Lofoten has received global media attention in international rankings of destinations.

4.4. Cross-case analysis

Table 2 summarizes the main findings regarding transformation of menus and experiencescapes into experience concepts but also how the concepts have influenced the destinations.

The target groups for the three cases are tourists; one focuses on children, another on bus tourists and the third on conference groups. When comparing the three cases, we found common denominators linked to the aspects in the consumer experience model (Mossberg, 2007, 2008). The first one refers to the product and quality-controlled standardized/set menus provided for a large number of visitors. The menus are based on local culinary heritage, local traditions and local food products and are linked to a story. The second denominator is the personnel, who act as storytellers and enhance the consumers' experience. In Astrid Lindgren's World and the Arn project, the personnel link the menus to the stories. At the Thon Hotel, the serving staff and chefs act according to a script and perform various roles in the show. One specific performer guides the guests from the start to the end of the meal.

The third denominator is the experiencescape, which is linked to the story but in different ways. In Astrid Lindgren's World, the restaurants' indoor and exterior décor is related to Lindgren's books and characters. The theme park is located close to the area where Astrid Lindgren was born and most of her stories take place. As for Arn, nothing from the story can be recognized inside the venues. However, the story of Arn is connected geographically to the locations of the restaurant and café. Two of the medieval churches mentioned in the books are situated next door to the facilities. Thon Hotel Lofoten uses

Table 2. Across cases – an overview of findings.

Case	Transformation of menus into meal experience concepts	Transformation of experiencescapes	Influence of meal experience concept on destinations
Astrid Lindgren's World	Change of target group with focus on children. Removal of fast food. Development of quality-controlled meal experience concepts related to Astrid Lindgren's books. Standardized and set menus based on local cultural heritage and local food products. Personnel link the menu to the story.	The interior and exterior designs of the restaurants and cafés are linked to the park's overall theme or the subthemes. The park is located in a geographical area connected to the story.	The theme park is a magnet for the destination. New meal experience concepts increase cooperation and support of local businesses. The meal experience concepts resulted in considerable media attention.
Arn	Change of target group with focus on pre-booked bus tours. Development of different types of quality-controlled meal experience concepts related to the Arn story. Set menus based on local cultural heritage and local food products. Personnel link the menu to the story.	The interior décor in the restaurant is not linked to the Arn story. The restaurant is located in a historical area connected to the story.	The Arn story became a magnet for the destination and inspired many stakeholders to take part in the offerings. New meal experience concept increased cooperation and support of local businesses. The meal experience concept resulted in media attention.
Thon Hotel Lofoten	Change of target group with focus on pre-booked conference groups. Development of various meal experience concepts connected to Lofoten and fishing. Set menus based on local cultural heritage and local food products. Personnel act according to a script and perform roles.	The interior décor where the staged meals are conducted is temporarily designed to fit the story but the rest of the hotel is not. The location in the harbour brings the Lofoten nature, culture and locals close.	The conference facilities and the meal experience concepts are magnets for the destination. The new meal experience concepts increase cooperation and support of local businesses.

ordinary conference rooms or an auditorium for its shows depending on the size of the group. By projecting films and pictures on the walls and by playing music following the script related to Lofoten fishing and nature, the room is temporarily transformed. The hotel is located directly adjacent to the sea, that is, to the context of the story.

The three meal experience concepts have all contributed to the destinations with increased visitation rates, more cooperation among businesses and significant media attention.

5. Discussion and conclusion

The aim of this study is to explore, from an experience staging framework, how storytelling can be used to develop meal experience concepts. Three cases were chosen: two Swedish based on stories from literature and film and one Norwegian related to spectacular meals for large groups with stories based on coastal culture.

The first goal is to analyse the transformation of menus into experience concepts and dining areas into experiencescapes. The study shows how narrative staging of menus can facilitate a consistent experience concept in restaurants. In Astrid Lindgren's World in Sweden, the overall food strategy is to serve nutritious food based on local resources and with a link between the menus and author Astrid Lindgren's books. One of the main restaurants connected to Arn offered a set Arn menu based on local food products. The spectacular dinner shows at Thon Hotel in Svolvaer offer a contrast not only to what is normally offered at a chain hotel but also to what food products are available in Lofoten. The visitors are transported back in time and encounter the contrast between the old and the modern life. All the restaurants connect to Nordic cuisine as they use local food products and point out the freshness and seasonality (Sundbo et al., 2013). The degree of freedom for the guests is limited as the restaurants offer standardized/set menus to be able to stick to their respective concepts and control the quality of their offerings. This makes them highly efficient and enables them to offer meals to a large number of guests in one day. The menus do not have to be very advanced and sophisticated as shown in Astrid Lindgren's World and in Arn. The menus correspond to what Therkelsen (2016) requested in her study of German tourists as they liked to experience country-specific meals to achieve a sense of place.

The narrative staging of the menus colours the experiencescape, which enhances its meaning through consistency, something that has earlier been pointed out as meaningful for consumer experiences (Mossberg, 2008). The overall story at, for example, Astrid Lindgren's World becomes a consistent total experience with a clear theme easy to connect to for Scandinavians since most children read Astrid Lindgren's books and identify with the themes in the park. The connection to the medieval time is obvious in the Arn case as the churches, monasteries and other historical buildings utilized are from that time period. In Lofoten, the economy has been built around fishing during a long period of time and the destination is strongly connected to the fishing tradition. The offerings are part of an emerging experience economy and the restaurants surely follow strategies pointed out in the experience staging literature about engaging the consumer symbolically (Pine & Gilmore, 2013). It is not only narrative add-ons to food products (Manniche & Larsen, 2012) as the narratives encompass the whole meal experience.

The second goal is to investigate if storytelling activities in restaurants can lead to destination development. The study gives an understanding of how narrated meals can strengthen not only the creative experience concepts of restaurants but also the destinations as such. A general problem for tourism organizations is the ease of copying good ideas. A unique story linked to a place is hard to copy, and if the concept is based on local food products and a local culinary heritage, it might be even harder. It is just not relevant to copy concepts such as the Arn menu to other places that lack a credible connection. A commercial, narrative environment was created at the three destinations where numerous stakeholders were involved. The process-oriented theoretical model suggested in another Nordic study proclaims the significance of strong leadership and stakeholder participation (Mossberg et al., 2010). The image of the theme park, from many stakeholders' point of view, has been strengthened because of the new food strategy. Media has brought attention to this development and the offering of local food products in the area has increased. Arn definitely increased the attraction of the restaurants, but it was also the other way around: the attractiveness of the whole Arn product increased because of the Arn-related meals served. The number of visitors increased and the cooperation among local businesses was strengthened. The dinner shows in Svolvaer serve as a magnet for the destination. This type of show is unique for Northern Norway and Lofoten and is sometimes used as a primary reason to visit the area. To increase the attractiveness of the hotel and to be able to offer visitors various types of activities, the hotel is actively trying to involve other firms that provide tours related to hiking, biking, climbing, fishing and culture. Some of them have also increased their business as a result of the shows. The three cases are characterized by strong leadership and cooperation among relevant stakeholders.

Spaargaren (2011) and Pine and Gilmore (2013) argue that consumption patterns can be changed when consumers get reminded about a recurring theme by intense interaction rituals. We suggest that restaurants can be an agent of change if they create business models which fit the sustainability trend and the logic of experience offerings with experience staging and storytelling. We also suggest that the use of experience staging as a theoretical framework can lead to a better understanding of Nordic food and food transformation in several ways.

First, stories speak to our human needs and transfer values and principles. Consumers in the three cases are offered stories which can be used as a source to make sense. The development of using local culture and culinary resources in storytelling of local food products is not just a dubious marketing activity; it is 'the heart of value creation in the new food economy' (Manniche & Larsen, 2012, p. 402). As stories involve us they can be used strategically in restaurants with an intention to facilitate healthy eating. One example is from Astrid Lindgren's World where a recipe of Pippi's pancakes is given away. The children can identify themselves with the story characters and should be reminded of the visit when they are back home and ask for Pippi's pancakes as well as other dishes linked to the books. The overall food message in the park is to demonstrate healthier alternatives compared to fast food. Local products and culinary traditions are highlighted in the menus and for a reasonable price, large and diverse groups of tourists get a connection to the place by standardized, authentic and healthy meals which are linked to commercialized and popularized stories. The management has a clear philosophy about children's food patterns and wants to contribute to the debate in media and schools on sustainable food consumption. Another example is shown in the Norwegian case with signs on the buffet table at the Christmas show elevating local cheese, lamb and traditional ways of preparing fish. The products can make the local visitors proud of their own local heritage and make others curious to try.

Second, stories communicate knowledge. A good story can be told and retold with newly added value. The story can give credibility to the message and a good story stays in the consciousness (Mossberg, 2008). The restaurants in the study but also other well recognized restaurants, like Noma in Copenhagen, can, therefore, be seen as arenas for storytelling with opinion leading activities. Unique or different stories will spread by word-of-mouth and might as well generate media attention. The made-up stories in the three cases take place in an out-of-the-ordinary context, that is, in themed enclaves. For the consumer to be immersed, it is claimed that consumption should take place in a secure and themed enclave (Carù & Cova, 2007) where the consumer interprets the story and co-creates a unique value. The enclave must contrast with the consumer's everyday life and the experience must be out of the ordinary. These types of staged meals based on stories take place in hedonic settings and are often perceived as extraordinary by the consumers. Extraordinary experiences are intense, joyful, often remembered and something consumers like to talk about and recommend to others.

Third, stories amuse and give attention. The framing of the experiencescape give consumers opportunity to be transported into imaginary worlds of pleasure, enjoyment and entertainment. During the dinner/Christmas shows in Lofoten many dramaturgical effects are used, which influence all the senses of the consumer. Besides the link to the menu, the storytelling activities in the Arn case occur foremost outside the restaurant when the consumer gets an authentic touch when visiting the nearby church connected to the Arn story. In Astrid Lindgren's World the whole experiencescape is framed by the narrated worlds. The experiencescape should be thought of as a commercial place where producers and consumers interact and where stories are negotiated, shaped and transformed (Chronis, 2005). A precondition for narrative transportation is that stories are easily understood by the target group, easy to connect to and to communicate (Van Laer et al., 2014). The target groups in the three cases need a pre-understanding of the storyline in order to create meaning when encountering the Astrid Lindgren World, the medieval history of Arn and the natural and cultural wonders of Lofoten when visiting the respective experiencescapes. If the consumers can empathize with the story, its characters and its food, they can experience a unique meal. Otherwise, the concepts do not make sense. For visitors outside the sociocultural sphere, it is hard to connect to the story. This was obvious when East African visitors to Lofoten attended a dinner show. They could not understand the story and were offended by some of the jokes carrying religious undertones. It is not only about fact or fantasy; it is also about trust, meaningfulness and involvement (Van Laer et al., 2014).

In general restaurants capture new trends, media notes the new concepts and consumers like to try what is novel and trendy. Nordic media has over the last decades put light on food experiences from various perspectives with for example comprehensive exposure of famous chefs and cook books with a quest to find the latest impulses. Consumers' frequent reading about the latest food trends, their participating in food festivals, their continuous searching for the most hip restaurants and so on shape consumption routines. We claim, in order to be successful, that restaurants have to take into account the sustainability trend with local produce and healthy food when staging the experiencescape. Otherwise the concepts will not be accepted by food enthusiasts who connect 'correct' food to their identity and who are important opinion leaders in food debates (Andersson & Mossberg, 2014). The overall goal of experience staging is to involve consumers. Storytelling in restaurants creates meaning and involves consumers. In general, highly involved consumers are important as agents of change. Therefore, consumers' visits to experience and sustainability staged restaurants can become turning points for more healthy food preferences in everyday life.The continues flow of staged meal concepts can be part of a transformation process which contribute to more sustainable, socially fair and healthier directions in the years to come.

More research is needed to further investigate the content and dramaturgical structure of stories and their impact on consumers, organizations and destinations. One issue to explore in further research is the border between ordinary and out of the ordinary in the context of meals. Novelty and uniqueness are fundamental when creating meal concepts but when are these types of activities perceived as ordinary?

Disclosure statement

No potential conflict of interest was reported by the authors.

Funding

This work was supported by The Research Council of Norway through the project Northern Insights: Service Innovation and Tourist Experiences in the High North; 195306.

References

Andersson, T., & Mossberg, L. (2014). Interest in food events: Some insights from Swedish consumers. In A. Cavicchi & C. Santini (Eds.), *Food and wine events in Europe – a stakeholder approach* (pp. 201–212). Routledge Advances in Event Research Series. New York, NY: Routledge.

Arnould, E., & Price, L. (1993). River magic: Extraordinary experience and the extended service encounter. *Journal of Consumer Research, 20*(June), 24–45. doi:10.1086/209331

Arnould, E., & Thompson, C. (2005). Consumer culture theory (CCT): Twenty years of research. *Journal of Consumer Research, 31*(4), 868–882. doi:10.1086/426626

Badot, O., & Filser, M. (2007). Re-enchantment of retailing: Toward utopian islands. In A. Carù, & B. Cova (Eds.), *Consuming Experience* (pp. 166–181). New York: Routledge.

Bessie're, J. (1998). Local development and heritage: Traditional food and cuisine as tourist attractions in rural areas. *Sociologia Ruralis, 38*(1), 21–34. doi:10.1111/1467-9523.00061

Carù, A., & Cova, B. (2007). Consumer immersion in an experiential context. In A. Carù, & B. Cova (Eds.), *Consuming experience* (pp. 34–47). London: Routledge.

Cavicchi, A., & Santini, C. (Eds.). (2014). *Food and wine events in Europe – a stakeholder approach*. Routledge Advances in Event Research Series. New York, NY: Routledge.

Chronis, A. (2005). Coconstructing heritage at the Gettysburg storyscape. *Annals of Tourism Research, 32*(2), 386–406. doi:10.1016/j.annals.2004.07.009

Crang, P. (1997). Performing the tourist product. In C. Rojek, & J. Urry (Eds.), *Touring cultures: Transformation of travel and theory* (pp. 137–154). London: Routledge.

Delgadillo, Y., & Escalas, E. J. (2004). Narrative word-of-mouth communication: Exploring memory and attitude effects of consumer storytelling. In B. E. Kahn & M. F. Luce (Eds.), *Advances in consumer research* (Vol. 31, pp. 186–192). Valdosta, GA: Association for Consumer Research.

Du Rand, G., Heath, E., & Alberts, N. (2003). The role of local and regional food in destination marketing: A South African situation analysis. *Journal of Travel and Tourism Marketing, 14*(3/4), 97–112. doi:10.1300/J073v14n03_06

Escalas, J. E. (2004). Imagine yourself in the product. Mental stimulation, narrative transportation, and persuasion. *Journal of Advertising, 33*(2), 37–48. doi:10.1080/00913367.2004.10639163

Firat, A. F., & Dholakia, N. (1998). *Consuming people. From political economy to theaters of consumption*. London: Routledge.

Flyvbjerg, B. (2001). *Making social science matter: Why social inquiry fails and how it can count again*. New York, NY: Cambridge University Press.

Gherardi, S. (2012). *How to conduct a practice-based study: Problems and methods*. Cheltenham: Edward Elgar.

Gottdiener, M. (1998). The semiotics of consumer spaces: The growing importance of themed environments. In J. F. Sherry (Eds.), *ServiceScapes* (pp. 29–54). Chicago, IL: NTC Business Books.

Guber, P. (2007). The four truths of the storyteller. *Harvard Business Review, 85*(12), 52–59.

Gustafsson, L. (2002). *Den förtrollande zonen: Lekar med tid, rum och identitet under medeltidsveckan på Gotland* (Dissertation). Stockholms Universitet, Nora: Nya Doxa.

Gustafsson, I.-B., Öström, Å., Johansson, J., & Mossberg, L. (2006). Five aspects meal model – a tool for developing meal services in restaurants. *Journal of Foodservice, 17*(2), 84–93. doi:10.1111/j.1745-4506.2006.00023

Hansen, A-H., & Mossberg, L. (2013). Consumer immersion: A key to extraordinary experiences. In J. Sunbo & F. Sørensen (Eds.), *Handbook on the experience economy* (pp. 209–227). Cheltenham: Edward Elgar. doi:10.4337/9781781004227.00022

Holbrook, M. B., & Hirschman, E. C. (1982). The experiential aspects of consumption: Consumer fantasies, feelings, and fun. *Journal of Consumer Research*, *9*(September), 132–140. doi:10.1086/208906

Hollenbeck, C., Peters, C., & Zinkhan, G. (2008). Retail spectacles and brand meaning: Insights from a brand museum case study. *Journal of Retailing*, *84*(3), 334–353. doi:10.1016/j.retai.2008.05.003

Kivela, J., & Crotts, J. C. (2006). Tourism and gastronomy: Gastronomy's influence on how tourists experience a destination. *Journal of Hospitality & Tourism Research*, *30*(3), 354–377. doi:10.1177/1096348006286797

Kozinets, R., Sherry, J., DeBerry-Spence, B., Duhachek, A., Nuttavuthisit, K., & Storm, D. (2002). Themed flagship brand stores in the new millennium: Theory, practice, prospects. *Journal of Retailing*, *78*(1), 17–29. doi:10.1016/S0022-4359(01)00063-X

Krizaj, D., Brodnik, A., & Bukovec, B. (2014). A tool for measurement of innovation newness and adoption in tourism firms. *International Journal of Tourism Research*, *16*(2), 113–125. doi:10.1002/jtr.1905

Kumar, V., & Karande, K. (2000). The effect of retail store environment on retailer performance. *Journal of Business Research*, *49*(2), 167–181. doi:10.1016/SO148-2963(99)00005-3

Lund, K. A. (2015). Magic mussels: Ingredients for improving a tourism destination. *Gastronomy and Tourism*, *1*(1), 19–32. doi:10.3727/216929715X14298190828831

Manniche, J., & Larsen, K. T. (2012). Experience staging and symbolic knowledge: The case of Bornholm culinary products. *European Urban and Regional Studies*, *20*(4), 401–416. doi:10.1177/0969776412453146

Miles, M. B., & Huberman, A. M. (1984). *Qualitative data analysis. A sourcebook of new methods.* Beverly Hills, CA: Sage.

Mossberg, L. (2007). A marketing approach to the tourist experience. *Scandinavian Journal of Hospitality and Tourism*, *7*(1), 59–74. doi:10.1080/15022250701231915

Mossberg, L. (2008). Extraordinary experiences through storytelling. *Scandinavian Journal of Hospitality and Tourism*, *8*(3), 195–210. doi:10.1080/15022250802532443

Mossberg, L., Therkelsen, A., Björk, P., Huijbens, E., & Olsson, A-K. (2010, December). *Storytelling and destination development.* Oslo: Nordic Innovation Center.

O'Dell, T., & Billing, P. (2005). *Experiencescapes: Tourism, culture, and economy.* Copenhagen, DK: Copenhagen Business School Press.

Okumus, B., Okumus, F., & McKercher, B. (2007). Incorporating local and international cuisines in the marketing of tourism destinations: The cases of Hong Kong and Turkey. *Tourism Management*, *28*(1), 253–261. doi:10.1016/j.tourman.2005.12.020

Pattersson, A., & Brown, S. (2005). No tale, no sale: A novel approach to marketing communication. *Marketing Review*, *5*, 315–328. doi:10.1362/146934705775186863

Peñaloza, L. (1999). Just doing it: A visual ethnographic study of spectacular consumption at Niketown. *Consumption, Markets and Culture*, *2*(4), 337–400. doi:10.1080/10253866.1998.9670322

Pine, B. J., & Gilmore, J. H. (1999). *The experience economy.* Boston, MA: Harvard Business School Press.

Pine, B. J., & Gilmore, J. H. (2013). The experience economy: Past, present, and future. In J. Sundbo & F. Sørensen (Eds.), *Handbook on the Experience Economy* (pp. 21–44). Cheltenham: Edward Elgar. doi:10.4337/9781781004227.00022

Quan, S., & Wang, N. (2004). Towards a structural model of the tourist experience: An illustration from food experiences in tourism. *Tourism Management*, *25*, 297–305. doi:10.1016/S0261-5177(03)00130-4

Shankar, A., Elliot, R., & Goulding, C. (2001). Understanding consumption: Contributions from a narrative perspective. *Journal of Marketing Management*, *17*(3/4), 429–453. doi:10.1362/0267257012652096

Shenoy, S. (2005). *Food tourist and the culinary tourist* (Ph.D. thesis). Parks, Recreation and Tourism Management at graduate School of Clemson University.

Sherry, J., Kozinets, R., Duhachek, A., DeBerry-Spence, B., Nuttavuthisit, K., & Storm, D. (2004). Gendered behavior in a male preserve: Role playing at ESPN Zone Chicago. *Journal of Consumer Psychology*, *14*(1&2), 151–158. doi:10.1207/s15327663jcp1401&2_17

Snel, A. (2011). *For the love of experience: Changing the experience economy discourse* (PhD dissertation). University of Amsterdam, Amsterdam.

Solér, C. (2012). Conceptualizing sustainably produced food for promotional purposes: A sustainable marketing approach. *Sustainability*, *4*(1), 294–340. doi:10.3390/su4030294

Spaargaren, G. (2011). Theories of practice: Agency, technology, and culture. Exploring the relevance of practice theories for the governance of sustainable consumption practices in the new world order. *Global Environment Change*, *21*, 813–822. doi:10.1016/j.gloenvcha.2011.03.010

Spaargaren, G., Oosterveer, P., & Loeber, A. (2012). Sustainability transitions in food consumption, retail and production. In G. Spaargaren, P. Oosterveer, & A. Loeber (Eds.), *Food practices in transition: Changing food consumption, retail and production in the age of reflexive modernity* (pp. 1–34). New York, NY: Taylor & Francis.

Stern, B. B., Thompson, C. J., & Arnould, E. J. (1998). Narrative analysis of a marketing relationship: The consumer's perspective. *Psychology & Marketing*, *15*(3), 195–214. doi:10.1002/(SICI)1520-6793(199805)15:3<195::AID-MAR1>3.0.CO;2-5

Story, M., Kaphingst, K., Robinson-O'Brien, R., & Glanz, K. (2008). Creating healthy food and eating environments: Policy and environmental approaches. *Annual Review of Public Health*, *29*, 253–272.

Sundbo, J., & F. Sørensen. (2013). Introduction to the experience economy. In J. Sunbo & F. Sørensen (Eds.), *Handbook on the experience economy* (pp. 1–17). Cheltenham: Edward Elgar. doi:10.4337/9781781004227.00022

Sundbo, J., Sundbo, D., & Jacobsen, J. K. (2013). Concept experiences and their diffusion: The example of the New Nordic Cuisine. In J. Sundbo & F. Sørensen (Eds.), *Handbook on the Experience Economy* (pp. 424–446). Cheltenham: Edward Elgar. doi:10.4337/9781781004227.00022

Svabo, C., Larsen, J., Haldrup, M., & Berenholdt, J. O. (2013). Experiencing spatial design. In J. Sundbo & F. Sørensen (Eds.), *Handbook on the experience economy* (pp. 310–324). Cheltenham: Edward Elgar. doi:10.4337/9781781004227.00022

Tellström, R., Gustafsson, I.-B., & Mossberg, L. (2005). Local food cultures in the Swedish rural economy. *Sociologia Ruralis*, *45*(4), 346–359. doi:10.1111/j.1467-9523.2005.00309.x

Tellström, R., Gustafsson, I.-B., & Mossberg, L. (2006). Consuming heritage: The use of local food culture in branding. *Place Branding*, *2*(2), 130–143. doi:10.1057/palgrave.pb.5990051

Therkelsen, A. (2016). Taking stock of the new Nordic cuisine at Danish coastal destinations. *Journal of Gastronomy and Tourism*, *2*(1), 15–25. doi:10.3727/216929716X14543659433777

Van Laer, T., de Ruyter, K., Visconti, L., & Wetzels, M. (2014). The extended transportation-imagery model: A meta-analysis of the antecedents and consequences of consumers' narrative transportation. *Journal of Consumer Research*, *40*(Feb), 797–815. doi:10.1086/673383

de la Ville, V. I., Brougère, G., & Boireau, N. (2010). How can food become fun? Exploring and testing possibilities. *Young Consumers*, *11*(2), 117–130. doi:10.1108/17473611011065809

Warde, A., & Martens, L. (2000). *Eating out: Social differentiation, consumption and pleasure*. Cambridge: Cambridge University Press.

Woodside, A. G. (2010). Brand-consumer storytelling theory and research: Introduction to special issue. *Psychology & Marketing*, *27*(6), 531–540. doi:10.1002/mar.20342

The reinvention of terroir in Danish food place promotion

Szilvia Gyimóthy

ABSTRACT
This paper conceptualizes place branding narratives that mobilize local food and contemporary gastronomic trends by revisiting the notion of terroir (taste of place) as a strategic marketing asset. In particular, it explores how rural tourism destinations with little or no gastronomic heritage exploit the discourses of New Nordic Food to create a distinct sense of place. An extensive review of the literature identifies two conservationist strategies by which terroir narratives are constructed (accreditation and patrimonialization), neither of which fully captures the particular rhetorical approaches shaping the Nordic terroir. Drawing on empirical illustrations from Danish rural destinations, the paper argues that terroir can be reproduced and invented through manipulative rhetorical approaches and identifies two novel, transformational strategies framing terroir narratives (exoticizing and enterprising). The paper contributes with a conceptual model conceived through a unique combination of place-specific (typicality) themes and market-specific ideologies, which has the explanatory power to distinguish Nordic terroir narratives from earlier articulations of taste of place.

Introduction

Globalization has significantly changed regional gastronomic identities, putting local food on the strategic agenda of urban and rural tourism destinations. Regional specialties and dishes feature as unique sales arguments in place branding, as they function as a 'specific sensory window' (Telfer & Hashimoto, 2003, p. 158) into the culture, history and people of a place. Central to food place branding and positioning is a plausible narrative articulating the taste of place (*goût de terroir*) to enhance a distinct place identity. However, the exploitation of regional gastronomy and culinary heritage in place branding is relatively new in a Nordic context. It is not before the issuing of the New Nordic Cuisine Manifesto in 2004 and the subsequent Nordic Council programme Ny Nordisk Mad (New Nordic Food, 2004) that local food and the taste of place have come to the fore as a strategic branding asset in Scandinavia. The growing number of international media coverages and digital websites on Nordic food, Nordic cookery, Nordic cuisine and Nordic kitchen (Christensen & Povlsen, 2010; Munch & Ellern, 2015) has also spurred the interest of visitors and consumers for the Nordic terroir. Today, each of the seven regional tourism destinations in Denmark puts a strategic emphasis on food in their regional promotion. In a matter of a decade, a region without long-standing gastronomic heritage and refined artisanal history is now consolidating a competitive gastronomic identity in Europe.

This paper addresses the special issue theme (transition of food production and consumption) within the context of strategic place-making. Hence, the intended contribution of this paper is to explore and conceptualize how the emergent Nordic food transition affected the narrative construction and invention of Nordic terroir. Terroir narratives have been extensively described in the literature; however, a strong dominance and interest in Mediterranean cases led to a narrow focus on conservationist strategies. These regard gastronomic cultures evolving over generations and centuries, where terroir stories are nurtured by arguments of longevity and traditions. Such a perspective obviously lacks the capacity to explain the rhetorical approaches shaping the Nordic terroir, which was literally absent before 2004. The paper thus addresses the question: How to conceptualize Nordic place promotion strategies and terroir constructions? What particular rhetorical approaches and ideologies are used to position Nordic regions as food places against more established Mediterranean competitors? In order to address these issues, the current study offers a conceptual exploration and critique of the existing literature and identifies the direction of a more nuanced framework that can distinguish Nordic terroir narratives from earlier articulations of taste of place.

Outline of the paper

The literature review opens with a brief positioning of food place branding synergies, acknowledging the significance of the terroir as a discursive strategic asset, as well as the dominant rhetorical approaches in place branding. Driven by the objective 'How is the terroir concept re/constructed in place promotion strategies?' it identifies key themes along which terroir is defined in various theoretical contexts, drawing attention to underlying ideological agendas of conservationist approaches. Second, based on a rhetorical analysis of contemporary place branding initiatives in Denmark, it demonstrates that rural tourism destinations create a distinct gastronomic sense of place by exploiting the transformational discourses of New Nordic Food instead of conforming to terroir accreditation schemes. This is followed by a discussion contrasting traditional and inventive approaches of terroir constructions, developed into a more nuanced conceptual model capturing four ideal types of narrative strategies framing the terroir. Positioning the Danish empirical examples in the model, the paper concludes that the New Nordic Food movement stimulated novel ways and narrative agents to articulate the taste of place.

Literature review: food and place branding synergies

Rural regeneration and diversification strategies often embrace particular narratives and storytelling approaches to position local culture and society (Burnett & Danson, 2004). The strategies of positioning rurality are based on a commodification of local assets and identity in order to appeal for consumers in the cultural economy (Ray, 1998). Acknowledging the significance of contemporary consumer trends and market preferences, Ray (1998) proposes a typology of commodification strategies or modes, along which rural areas can create an identity (an attractive sense of place) to embark on new developmental trajectories. Mode I emphasizes the construction of a territorial identity, focusing on the valorization, accreditation and control of products connected to local culture and history. The construction of a new and distinct territorial identity may also take place through the commodification of cultural resources, which are targeted at external market preferences (Mode II). In contrast, Mode III refers to an internally focused, community-building strategy, which attempts to reinforce local identity, local patriotism and pride among citizens and local businesses. Mode IV may operate within each of the three other modes, by pursuing 'alternative' development paths, for instance, by returning to/recovering indigenous value systems.

The potentials of food place branding synergies have been extensively studied within tourism and place branding (Berg & Sevón, 2014; Bruwer & Johnson, 2010; Du Rand, Heath, & Alberts, 2003; Frochot, 2003; Hall, Sharples, Mitchell, Macionis, & Cambourne, 2003). In accordance with the commodification strategies described above (Ray, 1998), these scholars identify local food as a strategic asset to raise awareness and create a distinctive image in tourists' mind. Food is often intertwined with the social, cultural and natural characteristics of a specific region, and may lend its symbolic capacities to articulate place/destination identity (Lin, Pearson, & Cai, 2011). More specifically, Berg and Sevón (2014) identify three strategic areas of food place branding synergies. First, the local food industry can be promoted by emphasizing the place of origin of their products. Second, the identity of places can be amplified by preserving and reinvigorating local culinary heritage. Third, local food and culinary heritage can also be used to explicitly change the image of places, and position them as vibrant, cosmopolitan culinary destinations (ibid.). As such, food place branding is basically a persuasive communicative endeavour, in which various rhetorical approaches are used to enchant market perceptions of individual products and complex destination experiences.

Rhetorical practices in place branding

The use of rhetoric is essential in persuasive communication, such as place branding, as it can simplify, reorganize or deliberately manipulate place image constructions. The classic typology of rhetorical arguments goes back to Aristotle, differentiating among logos (arguments based on logical rationale), pathos (arguments appealing to emotions and empathy) and ethos (justifying arguments based on the perceived authority of the speaker). In a seminal paper conceptualizing organizational legitimacy and rhetorical practices, Suchman (1995) differentiates between two main rhetorical approaches: the conforming and the manipulating approach. A conforming approach entails 'playing by the rules', that is, when an organization seeks to attain legitimacy by complying with the existing institutional logic and standards in a specific field. For instance, Ray's (1998) first commodification strategy (Mode I), building on the valorization of local produce, is an example of the conforming approach, as individual products are subjected to control and certification schemes. The manipulating approach is used when an organization is unable to adapt to the dominant institutional logic, and hence will proactively manipulate its stakeholders' perception to achieve its goals. Void of documentable arguments, manipulative approaches are based on pathos or ethos and communicate persuasive messages through opinion leaders or mediatized events. Elbe and Emmoth (2014) adopted Suchman's framework of legitimation strategies to study destination management organizations' (DMOs') management of their stakeholders and found that there was often used manipulating rhetoric to persuade and mobilize support from diverse stakeholders. The distinction between conforming and manipulating approaches can be particularly useful to understand terroir narratives aiming at valorizing local produce.

Terroir narratives and the valorization of local produce

In order to address the narrative construction and consolidation of food places, we must acknowledge that the notion of terroir evolved from a narrow viticultural concept to a more fuzzy branding term. Terroir is an ambiguous and multifaceted concept, articulating the uniqueness of local produce by imbuing them with exclusive, quality-warranting connotations and properties. Rooted in the French word *terre* (soil), the term terroir was initially used to refer to the unique configurations of environmental conditions in a vineyard (microclimate, topography and soil), defining a characteristic taste of place, that is, *goût de terroir* (Halliday & Johnson, 1992). The terroir-specific character of a local produce is thus distinguishable through signature tastes, scents and flavours (Hughes, 1995, p. 114), and over time, connoisseurs have developed a shared perception of how food products from a given vineyard or meadow should taste. As such, terroir narratives are always embedded in arguments of *typicité* or typicality. The following sections review how arguments of typicality are framed in the literature and scrutinize two conceptual notions describing terroir strategies.

The accreditation strategy: demonstrating typicality and traceability

Terroir designations have played an important role to protect, promote and valorize local produce in Europe, in which the ideals of enduring and geographically well-delineated production play a central role. Vaudour (2002) describes the *goût de terroir* as collective taste memory, which develops and matures over generations, and hence is typical to geographically earmarked products. In France, for instance, terroir has been used as a branding device since the 1930s, where the AOC (Appellation d'Origine Contrôlée) schemes were developed to distinguish high-quality wines by tracing them back to one particular slope or farm (Whalen, 2009). Such labels not only guarantee the traceability of agricultural products, but also act as quality markers, adding extra market value through authentication (Gyimóthy & Mykletun, 2009). Globalization made terroir typicality accreditation increasingly popular (Ilbery, Morris, Buller, Moye, & Kneafsey, 2005), as provenance labels offer exclusive positional advantages for rural produce against non-labelled, industrial mass-produced foods. At the same time, canonical terroir designations are fixative and exclusive (Paxson, 2010), nominating certain products or preparation techniques as typical representatives of a place, while excluding others. Provenance labels are also administration-heavy and require compliance with rigid, institutionalized accreditation schemes and subject local producers to regular controls.

The patrimonialization strategy: invoking tradition and heritage

The unique *goût de terroir* is articulated not only through references to climatic and topographical conditions, but also by the ways in which humans harnessed those physical and environmental givens over time. Embedded in agricultural history and gastronomy, terroir definitions in Europe also encompass place-bound production methods and artisanal traditions related to harvesting, refining and storage (Solheim, 2015). For example, the fermentation technique *méthode champenoise* has been developed and exclusively used in Champagne. Terroir may also refer to a distinct regional culinary culture, entailing traditional recipes for cooking, presenting and serving local dishes. Southern European rural destinations such as Catalunya, Sardegna or Provence are known to strategically use history and gastronomic heritage (Hjalager & Corigliano, 2000). Once seen as a sign of poverty, old-fashioned and small-scale production methods and simple, rustic dishes are now repositioned as exclusive and superior gastronomic offerings (Larsen & Österlund-Pötzsch, 2015). This revalorizing phenomenon is labelled as heritagization (Bessière, 2013) or 'patrimonialization' (Frigolé, 2010), referring to a retrospective and nostalgic narrative strategy. This resonates with Ray's (1998) idea that the conservation and subsequent mercantilization of the authentic/traditional are a fundamental mode of commodification in the contemporary cultural economy.

Most tourism destinations follow the reactionary politics of place, by packaging their locality in enchanting, yet often ethnocentric narratives of deep-rooted historical heritage. Such place-making practices follow a similar template of radical particularization, and paradoxically lead to conformed touristic imageries around the globe. For instance, the Slow Cities accreditation is based on a conservationist endorsement of places 'untouched' by modernity, and simultaneously exploits the nostalgic charm to turn rural destinations into fashionable places to visit. The European designations of Protected Designation of Origin (PDO) Protected Geographical Indication (PGI) and Traditional Specialities Guaranteed (TSG) are embedded in a conservationist ideology, using cultural-historical as well as geographical qualifiers of typicality. This elitist perspective is also reflected in the UNESCO definition of terroir:

> A terroir is a geographically limited area where a human community generates and accumulates along its history a set of culturally distinctive features, knowledges and practices based on a system of interactions between biophysical and human factors. The combination of techniques involved in production reveals originality, confers typicality and leads to a reputation for goods originating from this geographical area and therefore for its inhabitants. The terroirs are living and innovative spaces that cannot be reduced only to tradition. (UNESCO, 2005)

While recognizing deep and enduring connections between human society and landscape, the definition above also proposes a perspective on terroir as dynamically evolving, rather than static and backward-looking. As Elton (2013) and Telfer and Hashimoto (2003) concur, terroirs are alive – constantly adapting and changing local food cultures. Terroir is conceived in the synergies among environmental conditions, cultural traditions as well as advances in production technologies and consumer trends. Amy Trubek (2008) suggests that terroir is a narrative that does not only facilitate the localization of a product geographically and historically, but also in a system of values and ideals. A more complex ideological perspective opens the potential for radically different narrative constructions of terroir. Nevertheless, these strategies have not been explored and described systematically, and the concepts of accreditation and patrimonialization are inadequate to fully capture the particular rhetorical approaches characterizing the emergence of the Nordic terroir.

Defining the conceptual gap: the overlooked potential of terroir engineering

In conclusion, commodification strategies have so far been conceptualized through their embeddedness in a local-rural context, described as accreditation (Ilbery et al., 2005) and patrimonialization (Frigolé, 2010). So far, scholars have not offered alternative frameworks to these two conservationist approaches. However, there also exist terroir constructions which are not necessarily bound to narratives of historical typicality as in Southern Europe. Wine-producing regions in the US or New Zealand may lack an established viticultural heritage, yet they pursue the construction of some kind of 'placeness' in their marketing strategies (Charters, 2010). Instead of conforming to storytelling based on local heritage, their promotion entails the generation of new, desirable place identities (commodity fetishes) through stories about human dimensions of the terroir, for instance, craftsmanship and local pride. As Paxson (2010) demonstrates in her study of American artisan cheese producers, alternative terroir narratives are underpinned by moral, ethical and health rationales and hence are qualitatively different from terroir claims based on traditions and history. In her view, terroir can be 'reversely engineered'; that is, defined through exclusive, artisanal products and ideologies, rather than being the qualifiers of local products themselves (Paxson, 2010). The mobilization of moral and ethical dimensions may be particularly relevant to understand contemporary practices of food place branding, as they target external markets (Mode II of commodification strategies) and comply with consumer-oriented rhetoric to increase the symbolic value of rural products.

Exogenous (market) agendas present new potentials for newly established artisanal food producers and regions with limited culinary heritage. The reverse engineering of terroir rests on an extroverted ontology of place (Massey, 1999), asserting that places are constructed through their ties with the outside world, and uniqueness is defined by a particular constellation of social relations and a diverse mix of cohabiting cultures. For instance, Macau's inimitable culinary identity is positioned as a fusion of Cantonese, Portuguese and Mozambique cuisines. This hybridity enables social, cultural and economic connections between the local and the global, bringing about asymmetric opportunities to create a 'unique' sense of place and to enhance the gastronomic identity and appeal of a place. Following the analogy that terroir determines not only the flavour but also the character of the local food, Hall and his colleagues contend that food tourism destinations are engineered as *touristic terroirs* (Hall, Mitchell & Sharples, 2003, p. 34). A touristic terroir is made up of a unique bundle of thematic tourism services and activities (such as wine routes, food festivals and dining events) that together capture the taste of a place along a combination of sensory, cultural and moral parameters. The touristic terroir thrives on expressive narratives (rather than label designations), sensitive to contemporary food consumption trends. Tourism organizations, media coverages, local community, entrepreneurs, the retail sector as well as consumers are all contributing to the circle of terroir representations, hence having a much wider effect than promotional activities undertaken by agrofood producers alone.

The rapid emergence of the Nordic terroir confirms Trubek's (2008) assertion that terroir is a narrative construction, in which local food and rural societies are represented in particular ways. In order to assess the novelty of Nordic food place brands constructions and 'terroir engineering', the next sections explore the invention of Nordic touristic terroir through a rhetorical analysis of selected empirical evidence from Denmark. On the basis of this empirical analysis, the identified conceptual gaps are revisited in order to create a framework that is adaptable to the Nordic context.

The invention of Nordic touristic terroir

This section charts the invention of the Nordic terroir in a Danish context. Based on an analysis of contemporary place branding initiatives from two coastal destinations, it demonstrates that the transformational discourses of New Nordic Food have inspired rural tourism destinations to create a gastronomic sense of place that is distinct from conformist approaches. The empirical examples are taken from two established coastal destinations in Denmark (Wadden Sea and the Island of Funen), entailing recent digital and printed place promotional material (websites, videos and printed brochures from 2015) issued by VisitDenmark, the two regional DMOs and local food networks.

Until recently, food and gastronomy have not played an important role in Nordic place-making strategies. In contrast to Mediterranean destinations, Nordic regions have been less remarkable in preserving and promoting a distinct gastronomic heritage for domestic and international markets (Mørch, 1996; Solheim, 2015). Taken together, Denmark, Sweden and Finland boast fewer traditional products with protected geographical indications than one Italian region alone (European Commission, 2016). For instance, Emilia-Romagna features no less than 31 PDO, PGI or TSG designations as opposed to Danmark (6), Sweden (8) and Finland (10). Large-scale agricultural innovations and effective production technologies are often held accountable for the lack of regional diversity (Solheim, 2015), and Hjalager and Corigliano (2000) argue that efforts invested in catering for local market demands resulted in a Danish cuisine defined by the left-overs from export products and a neglect of local food culture (in Mørch's terms, 'garbage kitchen'). Furthermore, it is also debatable whether distinct regional culinary identities ever existed in Denmark (Mørch, 1996). According to a comprehensive mapping of Danish regional dishes by Westergaard (1974), very few regions can document traditional specialties and typical recipes dating before industrialization:

> Compared to Southern Europe, the independence, inventiveness and variety shows in very modest ways in Danish fishing populations [...]. Along the entire Mediterranean coast there are a myriad variations of fish soup – every coastline uses its own combination of fish types and herbs [...]. Each area has for many generations kept on preparing its characteristic recipes. In Denmark on the other hand, the fishermen take only one kind of fish home and it is almost always the same ingredients that went into a fish soup (roots vegetables, herbs and spices), regardless of coast or type of fish. (Westergaard, 1974, p. 246, own translation)

Arguably, the emergence of a unique food culture in the Nordic region is a recent phenomenon that takes its inspiration from the Slow Food movement and contemporary food consumption trends. It became internationally known when a few entrepreneurial chefs in Copenhagen issued the New Nordic Cuisine Manifesto (2004), endorsing local, seasonal food foraged freshly from nature or produced sustainably on a small scale. Some analysts (e.g. Byrkjeflot, Pedersen, & Svejenova, 2013) attribute the reinvigoration of Danish cooking to the New Nordic Cuisine movement; however, the entrepreneurial development of innovative local food production started long before the Manifesto was issued. Already in the late 1990s, local food with an innovative twist was adopted as a differentiator by rural regions in Scandinavia and several Danish coastal destinations jumped on the bandwagon to position themselves as original and attractive places in a gastronomic sense. For instance, the invention of 'regional food' on the Danish island of Bornholm and the subsequent development of its place brand 'Gourmet Bornholm' have a history of over two decades (Manniche, Larsen, & Petersen, 2009).

The New Nordic Cuisine Manifesto exploited this and other local, bottom-up initiatives to substantiate and propagate an ideologically novel gastronomic trend. Apart from moralizing good taste, the manifesto also subscribes to ethical statements related to animal welfare, biodiversity and sustainable, collaborative rural development (Munch & Ellern, 2015). Consciously compatible with contemporary food discourses, New Nordic Food has become a coherent, internationally acclaimed gastronomic movement. The New Nordic Cuisine opens up for terroir-esque constructions of place narratives, which are entrenched in the emergent enterprising gastronomic culture, characterized by the passion and expertise of Nordic chefs. The touristic terroir in VisitDenmark's promotional video carries clear references to the ideological landscape and values of the New Nordic Cuisine:

> New Nordic Cuisine is quite literally about going back to the roots of Danish cooking. It's about getting out into the Danish landscape to forage for the best and most unusual ingredients: rosehips, buckthorns, mushrooms and herbs to develop a new taste. It's about experimenting and presenting exciting new ways of combining traditional ingredients. And of course, it's all about giving you the best taste and dining experience possible. (VisitDenmark, 2012)

The excerpt uses pathos (rather than rational arguments) by acclaiming an ongoing gastronomic movement and its noble objective to create a new taste by going back to utopian roots. As Larsen and Österlund-Pötzsch (2015) comment, this rhetoric is very similar to the French Nouvelle Cuisine movement in the 1960s, which also treasured fresh and locally produced foods. Instead of venerating the merits of culinary traditions and heritage, the Nordic Cuisine claims that healthy, sustainable and tasty food can be created through technological-artisanal know-how and experimentation. The focus is not on the authentication or patrimonialization of existing products or dining traditions, but on pioneering craftsmanship, foraging and culinary inventions. The Danish landscape is re-enchanted along two partially new story motifs: (1) a sensuous, uncultivated area 'out there' waiting to be discovered and (2) a cultivated, artisanal, neo-pastoral landscape.

A raw and sensuous terroir

Remote and isolated destinations in the Northern periphery are often building on images of a raw, pristine touristic terroir. The Wadden Sea on the Danish west coast is also relying on its unique climatic and topographical qualities to portray itself as harsh marshlands. In line with the slogan 'Magnificently Simple' (Storslået Enkelt) and with images of sweeping, wind-blown beaches, and flat marshlands, the regional DMO conveys the image of a wild, yet amazing rich natural environment (VisitSydvestjylland, 2016). Climatic and topographical terroir dimensions are emphasized in the depiction of its characteristic fauna and flora:

> The flora on Mandø is characterised by the vegetation having to endure the strong westerly winds that often rule in the flat landscape. Even so, you will find and exciting selection of plants inside as well as outside the dike, such as the edible succulent Glasswort that contains high concentrations of table salt and soda. (VisitSydvestjylland, 2015)

> The marsh is a distinctive and unique landscape. Lamb and cattle graze here of the salty grass and herbs that are full of flavor and healthy minerals turning the meat into delicatessen. Furthermore local herbs from the marsh and beaches can be used for cooking, contributing to an exotic Nordic feature in the dishes. (Sydvestjyske madoplevelser, 2015)

The harsh, windy and salty flatlands are brought into play to justify the typicality (Vaudour, 2002) of the Wadden Sea food products. However, there is confusion about assigning typicality to a particular location, as the promotional material refers to geographical indications inconsistently, by shifting between local, regional, national and even Nordic terms. Climate and microclimate are used interchangeably in the tourism promotional videos, where scientific explanations from botany and biology are drawn upon to define the Nordic taste as particular and exotic:

> New Nordic Cuisine draws on natural produce that thrives in a cool climate. Denmark's northern location makes the growing of apples and asparagus a challenge, verging on the impossible. The yield is smaller, but the produce has unique character and greater intensity of flavor. From a culinary perspective, the cold sea offers perfect conditions for fish and shellfish, making them grow slowly, but firmer in the flesh. Low salt levers give seafood a fine sweet taste. (VisitDenmark, 2012)

Although these excerpts use logos by referring to a scientifically argued causality between lower temperatures and sensory characteristics, the terroir is not geographically, but ideologically demarcated. On a secondary connotative level, the material is saturated with value judgements, by inferring a 'natural' relationship between slower and robust growth rates, high quality and better flavour:

> Life is enjoyed at a slower pace along the Wadden Sea. And that also applies to the livestock. The cattle in the marshlands are fattened slowly on a diet of salt marsh grass, marsh samphire and other salt tolerant herbs. The lambs that graze the dykes also grow at a slower rate as they must struggle to find food and keep warm. Such harsh conditions add flavor to the meat when it is served as delicacies in local restaurants. Local farmers allow their organic chickens to sleep at night and such natural production methods give the meat a much better structure and taste. Slow food in the true sense. (Sydvestjyske smagsoplevelser, 2015)

Slowness as a 'natural' way of life in and around the Wadden Sea is deliberately contrasted against 'a hectic, modern lifestyle' conducted by the targeted market segments of the destination – a fine example of manipulative rhetoric appealing to potential holiday visitors. The values of organic farming and animal welfare are embedded in the narrative to infer that ethically raised poultry tastes better. As Paxson (2010) notes, reversely engineered terroir is a commodity fetish, when typicality is constructed along cultural and moral definitions of naturalness. The destination's value proposition inscribes itself in a cosmopolitan consumer discourse, accentuating the market value of unhurried and unspoiled (i.e. sustainable) growth. Furthermore, the harsh conditions signalling vulnerability, disadvantagedness and struggle are aestheticized to an extent that they may contribute to an 'underdog' effect (small is beautiful), raising consumer empathy and propensity to visit (cf. Larsen & Österlund-Pötzsch, 2015).

The Nordic food culture is heavily mediatized and endorsed by gastronomic sections of lifestyle magazines or celebrity chefs and cooking programmes (Christensen & Povlsen, 2010; Miele & Murdoch, 2002). The promotional websites of Danish destinations also feature trailers from BBC's international series about Nordic Cookery, featuring foodie experiences such as oyster safari, gourmet kitchen gardens as well as visits to local dairies and breweries. However, there are no explicit referrals to PGI-designated products (e.g. Vadehavslam and Vadehavsstude) in the portrayals of the Wadden Sea region's pulsating gastronomy. Local culinary traditions are given little attention, although it is briefly mentioned that the local dishes Sakukk and Bakskuld are listed in the 'Ark of Taste' (a gastronomic authority hardly known outside of Denmark). There are vague referrals to prehistoric or Viking foraging cultures, substantiating the 'back-to-the-roots'-credo of New Nordic Food. This implies that not only climatic and topographical particularities are engineered reversely, but also local, artisanal food production cultures.

Artisanal and neo-pastoral terroir

Danish food place narratives illustrate a terroir in the making, in which the eco-ethical ideologies of the Nordic Cuisine movement and local entrepreneurs play a prominent role. Several destinations use ethos as expert endorsement strategy, featuring appreciative videos with international and Danish celebrity chefs (e.g. Claus Meyer). Instead of accreditation schemes and provenance labels, stories of artisanal traditions, local patriotism and vocational passion become signifiers of the new terroir:

> Southwest Jutland is a true food mecca driven by enthusiastic local entrepreneurs, proud traditions of craftsmanship and a love of local ingredients. Old dairy traditions, ecology and local produce are quality markers that you will encounter again and again. Green spaces, the fresh westerwinds and proud traditions of craftsmanship are the ingredients of Southwest Jutland culinary creativity. (VisitSydvestjylland, 2015)

While the island of Bornholm, Mid-Jutland and Southwest Jutland take pride in their new gastro-craftmanship clusters, the island of Funen revives its culinary heritage as solidly grounded in peasant gastronomy, simple dishes and grandmother's cooking traditions. VisitFyn calls upon the heydays of pre-industrial agricultural production from the nineteenth century, by implicitly referring to the fairytale universe of Hans Christian Andersen:

> Among lavender and hollyhocks in a charming village with half-timbered houses with thatched roof, you are invited to probably the best dining experience in Denmark. Falsled Kro in idyllic South Funen is a gastronomic time pocket – where time goes at its own pace in the 200 years old restored premises. (VisitFyn, 2015)

Stories of grandma's kitchen and homemade products bring associations of cosiness, conviviality and community (Larsen & Österlund-Pötzsch, 2015) and a bygone lifestyle in the countryside. Paradoxically, the processes by which local culinary heritage is mobilized and reinvented for lifestyle consumption are strikingly similar in rural areas of Europe (Gyimóthy & Mykletun, 2009), and the embraced nostalgic stereotypes are increasingly at odds with industrial farming realities. The gastronomic time pocket offers an illusion of a sheltered enclave from fast food and globally distributed products. To make this fairytale setting plausible, potential visitors are lured by the opportunity of meeting 'real' locals (hosts, farmers and citizens) in these neo-pastoral landscapes. Funen's rural romance is further justified by adhering to the Slow Cities movement and its eco-ethical storytelling:

> You can taste that there are people, not machines who stand behind the production, perfectly suited to our Cittáslow philosophy. You can often buy farm produce directly from the source, at roadside booths, a particular characteristic of Funen. […] The local dairy host can tell you

the story about how the cow is chewing cud and the particularities of its cheese. (VisitFyn, 2015)

Both Funen's and the Wadden Sea brand narrative are constructed as a desirable touristic terroir for the food interested visitor, shaping a whole gastronomic universe ready for consumption. The Wadden Sea region promotes food experiences as exclusive culinary adventures, such as beach safaris and gourmet restaurants, while the Funen gastronomic culture is mostly packaged in the form of folksy events and communitarian encounters. Such examples are the farmer's markets and Danehof, which is a re-enactment of a medieval market and jousting in Nyborg Castle. More recently, Funen also launched three culinary routes, connecting small producers and places of interest along the themes of wine, chocolate and beer. The destination promotional material recommends to sample the biggest artisanal food brands (Løgismose/dairy products, Summerbird/chocolate and Skarø/birch syrup ice cream) as typical must-haves from Funen. Neither of these firms can be considered as 'underdogs' today, but their size is simply overlooked in favour to their modest start-up biographies (i.e. 'once they were small'). Their specialties are of recent origin and have never been a part of Funen's culinary heritage; yet, these are the very products that spearhead the new gourmet routes and events. Hence, it can be claimed that the neo-pastoral touristic terroir (simple, safe and tasty food) is constructed with consumer preferences and contemporary sponsors in mind, rather than based on historical recipes and authentic dining traditions.

Discussion: the revalorization of places as food destinations

The New Nordic Cuisine movement has given a new impetus and rationale to reinvent the gastronomic sense of place, paving the way for commodification strategies that are fundamentally different from the Southern European and Mediterranean food destination branding. It is positioned along hybrid ethics, claiming to unite gourmet taste with responsibility and reflexivity. Instead of conforming to canonized terroir constructions fixed in accredited provenance labels or signature heritage dishes, Danish food place promoters employ narrative strategies in which terroir is more dynamic and nebulous. The Nordic touristic terroir does not define a micro-region; its novelty lies in 'reversely engineered' consumer/market-focused brand narratives. Destinations subscribe to the transformational ideology of the New Nordic Cuisine Manifesto, which reiterates narratives about authenticity, simplicity and locally sourced produce, as well as moral imperatives about purity and freshness, ecology, health and well-being. Seen from this perspective, provenance is more ideological than cartographical and ethics and passion are replacing tradition and history as qualifiers. Destination narratives emerging in the wake of the New Nordic Food movement employ a manipulating rhetoric to persuade potential visitors of their significance as a food place brand (as they cannot comply with a rich culinary heritage and a multitude of designated terroir-specific products).

It is then possible to draw a conceptual model identifying four ideal types of narrative strategies framing the touristic terroir, by juxtaposing typicality arguments with ideological positions (Figure 1). Each of these strategies is conceived through a unique combination of place-specific (typicality) themes and market-specific ideologies. On the vertical axis, we can differentiate between geographical (natural, climatic and

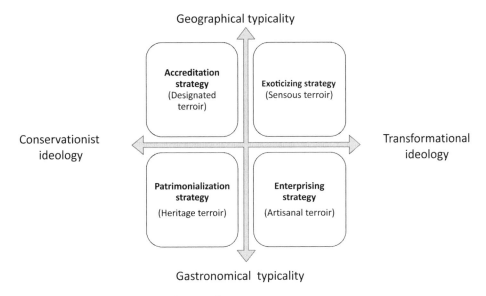

Figure 1. Four narrative strategies framing the touristic terroir.

topographical) typicality and gastronomical (food culture) typicality. On the horizontal axis, we can identify conservationist vs. transformationist ideology, adopting, conforming and manipulating rhetorical approaches, respectively. As such, the four terroir construction approaches entail Accreditation (i.e. the objective compliance with geographical indications and labels), Patrimonialization (the revalorization of culinary heritage and traditions), Exoticizing (the rediscovery and foraging of local flora and fauna for culinary innovations) and, finally, Enterprising (the celebration of emerging gastronomic clusters and craftsmanship).

The four approaches differ in terms of rhetorical approaches, strategic story motifs, gastronomic mediation and agency. The two strategies on the left-hand side (accreditation and patrimonialization) take their point of departure in a conforming rhetoric and conservationist ideology, highlighting 'earned' designations and heritage nominations by national or international authorities. The focus of these strategies is on demonstrating the exclusivity of labelled products and/or specific dishes and dining traditions, which are to be demarcated, fixed and controlled as terroir-specific. On the other hand, exoticization and enterprising take a more open and transformational approach where the authenticity of the terroir is justified with ethos and pathos (arguments based on opinion leaders and emotions). The focus of these strategies is on claiming the exclusivity of potentially new, exotic ingredients and/or artisanal movements. They unite the drivers of previously incompatible regimes into a warm, positive, yet fuzzy ideology – those of entrepreneurial ingenuity and passion, sustainability and sensory experiences. The focus of these last two strategies is to colonize an uncultivated foragescape and/or to evangelize an artisanal culture – both adopting a more extroverted and dynamic perspective on terroir. As demonstrated in the brief illustrations, it allows for new configurations that may transgress the traditional boundaries between urban/rural, local/global, traditional/trendy and authentic/invented and create hybrid imaginaries embracing both extremes of such dichotomies.

Implications for further research

The proposed typicality-ideology framework can be valuable for future studies of rural place branding narratives and identifying particular (conservationist vs. transformational) terroir constructions. More specifically, subsequent analyses can be structured and operationalized along the following concepts:

- Justification of typicality – documented vs. inferred
- Rhetorical approach – manipulative vs. conforming
- Themes of geographical typicality claims (climatic, topographical and environmental conditions)
- Themes of gastronomical typicality claims (culinary heritage, food traditions and contemporary food culture trends)
- Type of terroir (designated, heritage, sensuous or artisanal)
- Commodification object/medium of terroir (raw materials, processed food, recipes and community)
- Place brand brokers (food producers, retailers, DMOs, media and local community)

Implications for regional tourism/food promotion

In a video about the Nordic gastronomic wave, VisitDenmark underlines the place-making significance of New Nordic Cuisine, by claiming, that '[it] offers far more than pure taste: it's a new way of experiencing Denmark'. Considering the relative scarcity of objectively authentic (PGI-labelled) traditional food products in Denmark and the indistinctness of culinary heritage, tourism destinations are faced with a challenge when they want to strengthen their image as a culinary region. The cases of the Wadden Sea region and Funen demonstrate that New Nordic Cuisine offers new opportunities to reinvent their terroir or place-based taste, for instance, along the narratives of a harsh and primal pantry of nature or as neo-pastoral, cultivated gardens. Rather than relying on and reviving a few endangered or extinct dishes and recipes, Nordic regions ascribe significance to locally grown products and emerging local gastro-artisanship fuelled by contemporary food cultures and culinary innovations. A New Nordic-inspired food place identity is constructed along hybrid narratives, whereby various terroir elements (natural, cultural-historical and moral) are mobilized with a careful attention to market discourses. By adhering to a conformist, market-driven notion of what is typical and valuable and what is not, it can be argued that over time, even Nordic-invented terroirs may risk becoming largely similar.

If we take a closer look at how terroir is portrayed in Scandinavian tourism promotional material, it appears that the DMOs are struggling to imbue the grand narratives with inimitable substance. Confirming the observation of Charters (2010), the use of geographical earmarkers is inconsistent, where Nordic, Danish, regional and local provenance is claimed interchangeably. Void of protected designations as differentiators, positioning arguments are formulated along similar ideas, such as 'locally grown', 'high quality', 'seasonal produce', 'fresh fish', 'delicious apples', 'passionate chefs' and 'skilled producers'. These phrases are likely to originate from the recently established food networks, which define their identity through a set of common artisanship values. Also, the Nordic region abounds with undifferentiated food place brands, of which several claims to be 'the garden' (Funen, Denmark; Blekinge, Sweden) or 'the larder' (Hamar, Norway; Skåne, Sweden) of their country (Hamar Region, 2016; Sverigeturism, 2015; VisitFyn, 2015; VisitMittSkåne, 2016). The unique clichés of agricultural traditions and romantic countryside idyll are replaced with almost identical story motifs and pictures across Scandinavia, featuring the Nordic foragescape or playful and maverick gastronomic entrepreneurs (VisitDenmark, 2012; VisitIceland, 2016; VisitNorway, 2015; VisitSweden, 2016). There is a risk that the new terroir constructions may equally fall into the conformity trap (Antorini & Schultz, 2005), and fail to single out a distinct identity against more established culinary destinations.

A potential way out from the conformity paradox lies in reinforcing the specific touristic terroir, in which food is but one element of the rural or coastal experience (Therkelsen, 2016). The touristic terroir may be enacted through diverse brand touchpoints designed along the local context, for example, food-themed nature walks, historical festivals or stress-coaching courses, in which visitors may engage in a particular aspect of the local way of life. Furthermore, there is a solid opportunity in cross-appropriating different practices and contexts. Just as the culinary innovations of New Nordic Cooking reconfigure traditional and contemporary practices, the staging of coastal food experiences could also draw on urban and cosmopolitan inspirations. As demand for food tourism is becoming more diversified, a new competitive momentum can be gained through commodifying and exploiting contemporary connotations of local dishes and regional food, such as the Oyster Safari. This entails a reconstruction of the entire meal experience, rather than just aesthetically packaging traditional raw products, production methods and dishes or accrediting them with regional provenance labels.

Conclusion: the revalorization of places as food destinations

Addressing the transitional focus of the special issue, this paper studied the revalorization of rural areas through Nordic food-related discourses in tourism promotion. The implications of the Nordic food transition go far beyond agricultural production and food retailing. Rural place-making strategies in the North have undergone a fundamental shift in the past decade and there is a growing interest in Denmark, Sweden and Norway as gastronomic destinations. The invention of the Nordic terroir has reinvigorated rural tourism consumption, and hence transforming rural tourism production as well. The countryside is booming with new food festivals and gourmet routes passing by artisanal restaurants and organic farms. In the past five years, numerous international television productions contributed to the mediatization of Nordic regional cuisine and cookery. The multi-scalar and multisectoral impacts of New Nordic food suggest that it is not a marginal niche, but a more radical transition phenomenon that will continue to affect strategic priorities in the region's economy.

The paper opened with the question: 'How should we conceptualize Nordic place promotion strategies and terroir constructions?' and it contributes twofold. Based on an extensive literature review, it identified 'typicality' as one key dimension of terroir narratives, and pointed out the limitations of two crude strategic concepts in fully explaining the emergence and popularity of the Nordic terroir. To nuance and improve these unidimensional frameworks, the paper conceptualized terroir constructions by adding 'ideology' as another dimension and drew attention to transformational ideologies and manipulative rhetoric as alternatives to conservationist approaches. Empirically substantiated alternative strategies (exoticizing and enterprising) are particularly relevant to better understand the narrative engineering of the emergent Nordic terroir. The New Nordic movement contributed to innovative gastronomic identity transformations by tapping into contemporary ideologies and value systems of food consumption. Whereas the illustrations are solely based on Danish cases, the proposed analytical framework carries implications for food place branding at large and can inspire revalorization strategies in other rural and coastal areas in Europe.

Disclosure statement

No potential conflict of interest was reported by the author.

ORCID

Szilvia Gyimóthy http://orcid.org/0000-0002-1556-5632

References

Antorini, Y. M., & Schultz, M. (2005). Corporate branding and the 'conformity trap'. In M. Schultz, Y. M. Antorini, & F. F. Csaba (Eds.), *Corporate branding, purpose/people/process: Towards the second wave of corporate branding* (pp. 57–76). Frederiksberg: Copenhagen Business School Press.

Berg, P. O., & Sevón, G. (2014). Food-branding places – A sensory perspective. *Place Branding and Public Diplomacy*, 10(4), 289–304. doi:10.1057/pb.2014.29

Bessière, J. (2013). 'Heritagisation', a challenge for tourism promotion and regional development: An example of food heritage. *Journal of Heritage Tourism*, 8(4), 275–291. doi:10.1080/1743873X.2013.770861

Bruwer, J., & Johnson, R. (2010). Place-based marketing and regional branding strategy perspectives in the California wine industry. *Journal of Consumer Marketing*, 27(1), 5–16. doi:10.1108/07363761011012903

Burnett, K. A., & Danson, M. (2004). Adding or subtracting value? Constructions of rurality and Scottish quality food promotion. *International Journal of Entrepreneurial Behavior & Research*, 10(6), 384–403. doi:10.1108/13552550410564716

Byrkjeflot, H., Pedersen, J. S., & Svejenova, S. (2013). From label to practice: The process of creating new Nordic cuisine. *Journal of Culinary Science & Technology*, 11(1), 36–55. doi:10.1080/15428052.2013.754296

Charters, S. (2010, February 8–10). *Marketing terroir: A conceptual approach*. Paper presented at the 5th International Academy of Wine Business Research Conference, Auckland.

Christensen, D. R., & Povlsen, K. K. (2010). Mad, terroir og Tv:Smag på Danmark! *Mediekultur*, 45, 51–64. doi:10.7146/mediekultur.v24i45.512

Du Rand, G. E., Heath, E., & Alberts, N. (2014). The role of local and regional food in destination marketing. *Journal of Travel & Tourism Marketing*, 14(3–4), 97–112. doi:10.1300/J073v14n03_06

Elbe, J., & Emmoth, A. (2014). The use of rhetoric in legitimation strategies when mobilizing destination stakeholders. *Journal of Destination Marketing and Management*, 3(4), 210–217. doi:10.1016/j.jdmm.2014.08.001

Elton, S. (2013). *Consumed: Food for a finite platet*. Chicago, IL: University of Chicago Press.

European Commission. (2016). Geographical indications and traditional specialities. Retrieved from http://ec.europa.eu/agriculture/quality/schemes/index_en.htm

Frigolé, J. (2010). Patrimonialization and mercantilization of the authentic. Two fundamental strategies in a tertiary economy. In X. Roigé, & J. Frigolé (Eds.), *Constructing cultural and natural heritage: Parks, museums and rural heritage* (pp. 13–24). Barcelona: Institut de Recerca en Patrimoni Cultural de la Universitat de Girona.

Frochot, I. (2003). An analysis of regional positioning and its associated food images in French tourism regional brochures. *Journal of Travel and Tourism Marketing, 14*(3/4), 77–96. doi:10.1300/J073v14n03_05

Gyimóthy, S., & Mykletun, R. J. (2009). Scary food: Commodifying culinary heritage as meal adventures in tourism. *Journal of Vacation Marketing, 15*(3), 259–273. doi:10.1177/1356766709104271

Hall, M., Sharples, L., Mitchell, R., Macionis, N., & Cambourne, B. (2003). *Food tourism around the world. Development, management and markets*. Amsterdam: Butterworth Heinemann.

Hall, M. C., Mitchell, R., & Sharples, L. (2003). Consuming places: The role of food, wine and tourism in regional development. In M. Hall, L. Sharples, R. Mitchell, N. Macionis, & B. Cambourne (Eds.), *Food tourism around the world. Development, management and markets* (pp. 24–59). Amsterdam: Butterworth Heinemann.

Halliday, J., & Johnson, H. (1992). *The art and science of wine*. London: Mitchell Beazley.

Hamar Region. (2016). Velkommen til Hamarregionen – Norges spisekammer. Retrieved from http://norgesspiskammer.no/

Hjalager, A.-M., & Corigliano, M. A. (2000). Food for tourists – determinants of an image. *International Journal of Tourism Research, 2*(4), 281–293. doi:10.1002/1522-1970(200007/08)2:4<281::AID-JTR228>3.0.CO;2-Y

Hughes, G. (1995). Authenticity in tourism. *Annals of Tourism Research, 22*(4), 781–803. doi:10.1016/0160-7383(95)00020-X

Ilbery, B., Morris, C., Buller, H., Moye, D., & Kneafsey, M. (2005). Product, process and place: An examination of food marketing and labelling schemes in Europe and North America. *European Urban and Regional Studies, 12*(2), 116–132. doi:10.1177/0969776405048499

Larsen, H. P., & Österlund-Pötzsch, S. (2015). Islands in the Sun. Storytelling, place and terroir in food production on Nordic islands. *Ethnologia Scandinavica, 45*, 29–52. doi:10.1057/thr.2010.22

Lin, Y. C., Pearson, T. E., & Cai, L. (2011). Food as a form of destination identity: A tourism destination brand perspective. *Tourism and Hospitality Research, 11*(1), 20–48.

Manniche, J., Larsen, K., & Petersen, T. (2009). *Development and branding of 'regional food' of Bornholm*. Nexø: CRT.

Massey, D. (1999). Imagining globalization: Powergeometries of time-space. In A. Brah, M. Hickman, M. M. a. Ghaill, & M. Mac an Ghaill. (Eds.), *Global futures: Migration, environment and globalization* (pp. 27–44). New York: St. Martin's Press.

Miele, M., & Murdoch, J. (2002). The practical aesthetics of traditional cuisines: Slow food in Tuscany. *Sociologia Ruralis, 42*(4), 312–328. doi:10.1111/1467-9523.00219

Mørch, S. (1996). *Den sidste danmarkshistorie*. København: Det Danske Gastronomiske Akademi.

Munch, A., & Ellern, A.-K.B. (2015). Mapping the New Nordic issue-scape: How to navigate a diffuse controversy with digital methods. In Jóhannesson et al. (Eds.), *Tourism encounters and controversies: Ontological politics of tourism development. (New directions in tourism A nalysis)* (pp. 73–95). Abingdon: Routledge.

New Nordic Food. (2004). The kitchen manifesto. Retrieved from http://newnordicfood.org/about-nnf-ii/new-nordickitchen-manifesto.

Paxson, H. (2010). Locating value in Artisan cheese: Reverse engineering terroir for new-world landscapes. *American Anthropologist, 112*(3), 444–457. doi:10.1111/j.1548-1433.2010.01251.x

Ray, C. (1998). Culture, intellectual property and territorial rural development. *Sociologia Ruralis, 38*(1), 3–20. doi:10.1111/1467-9523.00060

Solheim, L. (2015). Det Danske Terroir. Retrieved from http://www.danskterroir.dk/

Suchman, M. C. (1995). Managing legitimacy: Strategic and institutional approaches. *The Academy of Management Review, 20*(3), 571–610. doi:10.2307/258788

Sverigeturism. (2015). Welcome to Blekinge, the garden of Sweden. Retrieved from http://www.sverigeturism.se/smorgasbord/smorgasbord/provincial/blekinge/welcome/se

Sydvestjyske smagsoplevelser. (2015). Lokale specialiteter fra Sydvestjylland. Retrieved from http://www.sydvestjyskesmagsoplevelser.dk

Telfer, D., & Hashimoto, A. (2003). Food for tourists in the Niagara region. The development of Nouvelle Cuisine. In M. Hall, L. Sharples, R. Mitchell, N. Macionis, & B. Cambourne (Eds.), *Food tourism around the world. Development, management and markets* (pp. 158–177). Amsterdam: Butterworth Heinemann.

Therkelsen, A. (2016). Taking stock of the New Nordic Cuisine at Danish coastal destinations. *Journal of Gastronomy and Tourism*, 2(1), 15–25. doi:10.3727/216929716X14546365943377

Trubek, A. B. (2008). *The taste of place. A culinary journey into terroir*. Berkeley: The University of California Press.

UNESCO. (2005). Planète Terroirs. Convention sur la protection et la promotion de la diversité des expressions culturelles, Paris.

Vaudour, E. (2002). The quality of grapes and wine in relation to geography: Notions of terroir at various scales. *Journal of Wine Research*, 13(2), 117–141. doi:10.1080/0957126022000017981

VisitDenmark. (2012). Learn about New Nordic Cuisine in Denmark. Video. Retrieved from https://www.youtube.com/watch?v=oIKV_X5ehWs

VisitFyn. (2015). Culinary Fyn – the garden of Denmark. Retrieved from http://www.visitfyn.com/ln-int/funen/gastronomy/culinary-fyn-garden-denmark

VisitIceland. (2016). Stay for the food. Retrieved from http://www.visiticeland.com/things-to-do/culture/dining

VisitMittSkåne. (2016). Skåne, Sveriges Spisekammer. Retrieved from http://www.visitmittskane.se/da/oplev/kultur/

VisitNorway. (2015). From birch to sea urchins: The distint flavors of modern Norwegian food. Retrieved from https://www.visitnorway.com/things-to-do/food-and-drink/the-taste-of-the-new-nordic-cuisine/

VisitSweden. (2016). Gourmet mad i Skåne – hele Sveriges spisekammer. Retrieved from http://danmark.visitsweden.com/aktiviteter/svensk-kultur/mad-og-drikke/

VisitSydvestjylland. (2015). Destination South West Denmark: From the tempestuous North Sea to idyllic towns. Press Release.

VisitSydvestjylland. (2016). Welcome to South West Denmark. Retrieved from http://sydvestjylland.com/da/home/

Westergaard, E. K. (1974). *Danske Egnsretter: Fra det Gamle Danske Køkken*. Viborg: Lindhardt og Ringhof.

Whalen, P. (2009). 'Insofar as the ruby wine seduces them': Cultural strategies for selling wine in inter-war burgundy. *Contemporary European History*, 18(1), 67–98. doi:10.1017/S0960777308004839

Index

Notes: Page numbers in *italics* refer to figures
Page numbers in **bold** refer to tables

abattoir technological systems 5, 75
accreditation, of terroir 103
agriculture: organic, challenges of 29–30; sustainable forms of 19
alternative food networks 1, 48, 69, 77 78
Andersen, Hans Christian 109
Anderson, J. C. 49, 51, 59, 61
Änglamark 55
AOC (Appellation d'Origine Contrôlée) schemes 103
Arn *see* regional museum, Skara (Sweden)
Arnould, E. 85
assistance effect 58
Astrid Lindgren's World 88, **89**, 93–6; cross-case analysis 92–3, **93**; culinary experience 89–90
Axelsson, B. 49

Berg, P. O. 102
Bessie're, J. 86
Biodynamic Products (BP) 34, 36
Biodynamiska Foreningen (Organic Association), Sweden 17
Bjørkhaug, Hilde 4, 47
Boltanski, L. 68
Bondens Marked (2016) 16
Born, B. 3
BP *see* Biodynamic Products (BP)
brewing industry 17
Brodnik, A. 88
broilers, organic 5, 74–6, **76**
Brunori, G. 77
Bukovec, B. 88

Campbell, H. 33
Carlsberg 17
Carù, A. 87, 88
certification, of food products 13, 17, 23
Charters, S. 112
climate change 30, 31; anthropogenic 29
Coenen, L. 3
consumer-oriented information 20–1

conventionalization hypothesis 33
convention theory (CT) 2, 67–9, 80
Cook, C. 49
Coop: Røros Dairy and 54–6, 55, 57, *57*, 58, 59-61
corporate food regime 4, 30, 33, 36, 40–3; transformation of 31–3
Cova, B. 87, 88
craft beer 67, 72–4, 76, **76**; and microbreweries 17–18
CT *see* convention theory (CT)

Danske Bryghuse 17
Denmark: brewing industry in 17; broilers 74, 75; coastal destinations in 106; consumers 67, 68; craft brewers 73; farm processing of food 15; food market 66; food system 66, 67–8; organic food 4, 16, 67; place branding initiatives in 101; rural tourist destinations 7; specialty food in 14–22
destination management organizations (DMOs) 102, 106
'DIY (Do It Yourself) mind-set' 78
drink industries 14, **14**

Easton, G. 49
Eide, Dorthe 6, 84
Ekolådan (EL), case study 34, 35–7
Elbe, J. 102
Elton, S. 104
Elzen, B. 42
Emerson, R. 49
Emmoth, A. 102
Esping-Andersen, G. 13
exogenous (market) agendas 105
experiencescapes 86–9, 92–4, **93**, 96
experience staging 85, 86, 93–6

farmers: KRAV-certified 34–5; market 16; organic 58
farmers' markets 16
farming *see* organic farming

INDEX

farm processing, of food 15
fermentation techniques, *méthode champenoise* 104
flour: markets, diversification of 71; specialty (case study) 70–2, 76, **76**
food: destinations for 110–11, 113–14; farm processing of 15; governance, Scandinavian model 4; industries 14, **14**; innovation in tourism and rural development 6–8; market changes 3–4; movement framework *31*; networks, alternative 1, 69, 77; in Nordic countries 8–9; place branding 100, 101; practices 30; products certification 13, 17, 23; promotion, implications 112–13; re-territorialization of 1; transition 2–3
food chains 47, 48
Food Communities 67
food quality 34, 67; transition of 69; understanding and analysing 68–9
food regimes *31*, 41; corporate 4, 30, 33, 36, 40–3; corporate, transformation of 31–3; current 8, 31; features of 35; hegemonic 33; industrial 6; progressive or radical 42
Food Strategy for Sweden (2015) 15
food system: conventional 78; embedding new quality aspects in 77–8; global 30; global, transformational shift in 40
food tourism 105, 113
food trends 5; in product categories 77–9; translating 77
Ford, D. 49

Gadde, L.-E. 49
Gästgiveri, Forshems 90
Geels, F. W. 32
Gherardi, S. 88
Gilmore, J. H. 95
Giménez, Holt 31, 33, 35, 41, 43
Glanz, K. 85
globalization 68, 100, 103
goût de terroir 100, 103
Guidi, F. 77
Guthman, J. 47
Gyimóthy, Szilvia 7, 100

Håkansson, H. 49, 52
Halkier, Henrik 3, 4, 8, 11
Hashimoto, A. 104
Healthy Growth project 47, 52
Hermansen, M. E. T. 68
Holmen, E. 51

IMP *see* industrial network perspective (IMP)
industrial network perspective (IMP) 48–52, 61, 62
industry *see specific types of industry*
Innovation Norway (IN) 53, 55, 59
interconnectedness 50, 56, 58, 61

James, Laura 3, 11
Johanson, J. 52

Kaphingst, K. 85
Kjeldsen, Chris 5, 66
KRAV 17, 19, 36, 38; -certified farmers 34–5; -certified products 38–9
Krizaj, D. 88
Kvam, Gunn-Turid 4, 47

Label Rouge system, France 74
Lantbrukarnas Riksförbund (LRF) 15
La Rocca, A. 61
Larsen, H. P. 107
Larsen, K. T. 84
local food 4, 7, 19, 24, 32, 34, 102, 105; consumer awareness of 21; culture 106; defined 15, 24; development 53; farm processing and 15; festivals 16; Norwegian development policy for 22; policies 23; prevalence of 13–14; products 7, 22, 88, 91, 92, 94, 95; from Røros 53, 60; sale of 15, 18; in Sweden 22; system model 37; tourist destinations with 21
local production 15, 103–4
'local trap', of food 3
LRF *see Lantbrukarnas Riksförbund* (LRF)

Manniche, Jesper 1, 84, 86
markets: development of 70; farmers' 16; firms and 4–6; food, changes to 3–4; food, in Denmark 66; initiatives 20–1; organic food 60, 62
Marsden, Terry 2, 68, 77–8
Matlandet Sverige 22
meal concepts 96
méthode champenoise, fermentation technique 104
microbreweries, and craft beer 14, 17–18, **18**, 23
Miles, R. 49
Milestad, Rebecka 4, 29
MLP *see* multi-level perspective (MLP)
Moragues-Faus, A. M. 68, 77
Mossberg, Lena 6, 84
Mount, P. 48
multi-level perspective (MLP) 31, 32, 43

network effects 49, 61
network identity 49, 51, 61, 62; dairy 60; definition 51; positive and negative effects on 51–2, 59–60
New Nordic Cuisine (NNC) 68; manifesto 1–2, 7, 100, 106–7; movement 110
New Nordic Food (NNF) 7, 11, 12, 68, 100, 107; movement 101, 110; multisectoral impacts of 113; -inspired place identity 112; transformational discourses of 101, 106
niche 4–6; impact on regime 41; micro-level 30; Organic 3.0 33; producers, challenges of 3
'niche within a niche' 30, 33, 41, 42
NNC *see* New Nordic Cuisine (NNC)
NNF *see* New Nordic Food (NNF)
Noe, Egon 5, 66
Nordic cookery 100, 108
Nordic Council programme 100

INDEX

Nordic cuisine 86, 94, 100, 107, 109
Nordic food 100; 108; transition 8–9, 101, 113
Nordic Genetic Resource Center (NorGen) 71
Nordic societies 8
Nordic terroir 101, 105; touristic 110, 106–7
NorGen *see* Nordic Genetic Resource Center (NorGen)
Norway: farm processing of food 15; local food development policy 22; Ministry of Agriculture and Food 20; organic food in 5, 16–17, 53, 62; retailers in 5; specialty food in 14–22

Økomat Røros *see* organic firms, influence of relationships
organic(s) 30, 33, **76**; agriculture, challenges of 29–30; broilers 5, 74–6, **76**; consumption, in Denmark 67; mainstream 4, 30, 40, 42, 54, 62; policies for 18–20; products 16–17
Organic Association 16, 17
organic chains, mid-scale values-based 48
organic farming 30; in Sweden 33–4
organic firms: destiny 62; identity 4; network identity 51, 59, 60; relationship 48
organic firms, influence of relationships 52–4; Røros Dairy and Coop 54–6, **55**, *57*; Røros Dairy and Innovation Norway 59; Røros Dairy and local customers 58; Røros Dairy and Matmerk 59; Røros Dairy and Norgesgruppen 58; Røros Dairy and organic farmers 58; Røros Dairy and Tine 57–8
organic food 14, 16, **16**, 47; demand for 67; in Denmark 4, 16, 67; food chains 47, 48; market 60, 62; movement 34; in Norway 5, 16–17, 53, 62; products 34; in Sweden 3, 4, 33–4;
organic food initiatives, case study: Ekolådan (EL) 34, 35–7, 40–2; Upplandsbondens (UB) 34–5, 38–42
organic initiatives 33, 40, 41, 53; in Sweden 4
Organic 1.0 initiatives 30
Organic 2.0 initiatives 30
Organic 3.0 initiatives 30, 33, 42–3
Österlund-Pötzsch, S. 107

patrimonialization 103–4, 105, 107, 111
Paxson, H. 105, 108
PDO *see* protected designation of origin (PDO)
Pedersen, Ann-Charlott 4, 47, 51
PGI *see* protected geographical indication (PGI)
Pine, B. J. 95
place branding 6, 7, 101–2; activities 2, 85; food 100, 101; initiatives in Denmark 101; rhetorical practices in 102–3; sales arguments in 100; synergies 101–2
policies: local and regional growth 21–2; for organics 18–20
Ponte, S. 69
Price, L. 85
producers: network creation between 13; quality-oriented 48

protected designation of origin (PDO) 15, **15**, 104
protected geographical indication (PGI) 15, **15**, 54, 104
public policy 18, 19; *see also* policies
Purcell, M. 3

quality conventions, in Danish food system 67–8
quality food 5, 12, 19, 21, 32, 34, 39, 40; organic 60, 62
quality turn 11, 68

Ray, C. 101, 102, 104
regional development policies 34
regional museum, Skara (Sweden) 88, **89**, 93–6; cross-case analysis 92–3, **93**; and culinary experience 90–1
regional producer networks 85
Ritter, T. 50, 56–9, 62
Robinson-O'Brien, R. 85
Røros Dairy *see* organic firms, influence of relationships
Røros Hotel 54, 60
Rosin, C. 33
Rossi, A. 77

Salais, R. 7, 68
Sæther, Bjørnar 1
Scandinavia 11; food approaches in 6; food governance 4, 24; organic food and drink in **16**; specialty food 11, 24; 'terroir' food in 2; 'transition' of food systems 2; welfare societies 13
Sevón, G. 102
Seyfang, G. 32
'sharewhare culture' 78
Shattuck, A. 31, 33, 35, 41, 43
Smagen af Danmark networks 21
Smith, A. 32
Smith, E. 77–8
Snehota, I. 49
Snow, C. C. 49
Sonnino, R. 68, 77, 78
Spaargaren, G. 85, 95
specialty foods 11, 13, 16, 24; conceptual framing of 12–13; in Denmark 14–18; farm processing and local production 15; flour (case study) 70–2, 76, **76**; market demand for 12; methodological issues 13–14; microbreweries and craft beer 17–18, **18**; in Norway 14–19; organic products **16**, 16–17; protected regional food labels 14–15; Scandinavian 11, 24; in Sweden 14–18
specialty food development 18–22; consumer-oriented information and marketing initiatives 20–1; local and regional growth policies 21–2; policies for organics 18–20
Spesialitet (specialty) 15, 54
Stockholm Beer Festival 17
Storper, M. 7, 68

119

INDEX

Story, M. 85
storytelling 84; and dialogue 6; drawbacks of using 87; eco-ethical 109–10; of local food products 95; meal experience concepts development 7, 93; in meal provision 6; in restaurants 86, 94, 96
Stræte, Egil Petter 3, 11, 68, 77, 78
Suchman, M. C. 102
sustainability transformation 29–30, 32, 40, 43
sustainable food systems 29, 33, 36
sustainable agriculture, forms of 19
Sverige Matlandet 19
Sweden: *Biodynamiska Foreningen* (Organic Association) 17; brewing industry in 17; Lantbrukarnas Riksförbund (LRF) 15; local food in 22; organics in 3, 4, 33–4; specialty food in 14–22
synergy effect (two-way positive effect) 58
Systembolaget 17

Telfer, D. 104
terroir 7, 104, 107–9; accreditation strategy 103; artisanal and neo-pastoral 109–10; dimensions, climate and topographical 107; engineering, overlooked potential of 104–5; *goût de terroir* 103; narratives 103–4; Nordic 105; patrimonialization strategy 103–4; *see also* touristic terroir
Therkelsen, A. 86, 94

Thevenot, L. 68
Thon Hotel Lofoten 88, **89**, 93–6; cross-case analysis 92–3, **93**; culinary experience 91–2
Thorsøe, Martin Hvarregaard 5, 13, 66
Three worlds of welfare capitalism (1990) 13
Tine 53; and Røros Dairy 57–8
Tine Råvare 53
tourism: food 105, 113; regional 6–8, 85, 112–13; and rural development 6–8
touristic terroir 105, 107, 110, 111, *111*, 113; neo-pastoral; Nordic 110, 106–7
traditional speciality guaranteed (TSG) 15, **15**, 104
transitions, food 2–3, 8–9, 69
Tregear, A. 77
Trubek, A. B. 105
TSG *see* traditional speciality guaranteed (TSG)
two-way positive effect (synergy effect) 58, 59
typicality 103–5, 108, 113

Upplandsbondens (UB) 34–5, 38–42

Vaudour, E. 103
Vinmonopol 17
von Oelreich, Jacob 4, 29

Wadden Sea food products 108
Waluszewski, A. 49
welfare societies, Scandinavian 13